Mastering JavaScript Promises

Discover and explore the world of promises, one of
JavaScript's most powerful concepts

Muzzamil Hussain

BIRMINGHAM - MUMBAI

Mastering JavaScript Promises

First published: July 2015

Production reference: 1210715

Published by Packt Publishing Ltd.
Livery Place
35 Livery Street
Birmingham B3 2PB, UK.

ISBN 978-1-78398-550-0

www.packtpub.com

Credits

Author
Muzzamil Hussain

Reviewers
Luca Mezzalira

Jebin B V

Commissioning Editor
Edward Gordon

Acquisition Editor
Meeta Rajani

Content Development Editor
Ajinkya Paranjape

Technical Editor
Siddhi Rane

Copy Editor
Janbal Dharmaraj

Project Coordinator
Harshal Ved

Proofreader
Safis Editing

Indexer
Priya Sane

Graphics
Sheetal Aute

Production Coordinator
Komal Ramchandani

Cover Work
Komal Ramchandani

About the Author

Muzzamil Hussain has been working in the field of computing/information technology for more than a decade now. During this period, he developed a wide range of software products and services for companies around the world.

He completed his Digital Communications Networks course from the prestigious London Metropolitan University, London, United Kingdom. He is skilled in crafting software products and services with the best of technical and management skills, which he has acquired over the past 14 years.

The best part of his wealth of experience is the dual skill sets of project management and software engineering, which is a paramount feature of his work.

Muzzamil has worked with some of the big industries based in Pakistan, the UK, the USA, Canada, and UAE. These days, he is associated with Systems Limited, the first and one of the oldest software companies in Pakistan, in the capacity of senior project manager.

He also provides consultancy to start-ups on the software development life cycle, project management, release engineering, and continuous integrations.

He is also heavily involved in experimenting with the latest technologies such as the MEAN stack, an opinionated full-stack JavaScript framework, and Apache Hadoop for the distributed processing of large data sets.

He blogs at `http://muzzamil.net/`.

There are several people I would like to acknowledge and thank everyone who helped me not only in writing this book, but also those who were an inspiration to my professional growth, making me a better person.

Thanks to all those amazing people around me: my father, Mr. Musharraf Hussain, and my mother, Mrs. Rifat Hussain, who raised me with their best resources and provided a healthy foundation for my life. My teachers, who not only educated me with their best skills and knowledge, but also made me understand the tough lessons of life. Finally, my wife, Amber Muzzamil, and my daughters, Abeeha and Aroush, whose continuous and unconditional support was the biggest factor in making this book a reality.

About the Reviewers

Luca Mezzalira is a passionate Italian software developer with more than 10 years of experience in frontend technologies, in particular, JavaScript, HTML 5, Haxe, Flash, Flex, AIR, Lua, and Swift.

He has often been involved in cutting-edge projects for mobile (iOS, Android, and Blackberry), desktop, web, and embedded devices too for big corporations.

He really loves his job and tries to apply the Kaizen culture of continuous improvement and the XP principles and values in his daily life.

He strongly believes that agile and lean methodologies can help you achieve any goal during your job, improving yourself and the people you are working with.

In his spare time, Luca learns new technologies and methodologies by reading books and attending meetup events or conferences. He is very flexible and adaptive to any situation, always trying to achieve great goals in the best way possible.

He has collected different certifications and acknowledgements across the last 10 years, such as Certified Scrum Master and SAFe Agilist; Adobe Certified Expert and instructor on Flash, Flex, AIR, and Flash Lite; Adobe Community Professional; and Adobe Italy Consultant.

He has written for national and international technical magazines and is a technical reviewer for Packt Publishing.

He speaks at national and international conferences and community events, such as Lean Kanban United Kingdom, Flash Camp, Scotch on the Rocks, 360 Flex, PyCon, and so on.

In his spare time, Luca likes to watch football, play with his dogs, Paco and Maya, and study new programming languages.

The first mention is for my family that always helps me, in particular, my parents who support and inspire me everyday with their strength and love. A big thanks to my brother, who is also one of my best friends. He is the most intelligent person that I've ever met in my life; his suggestions and ideas are very important to me.

Then, I really have a lot of other friends to say thanks to for what we have created together until now. I hope to not forget anybody: Piergiorgio Niero, Chiara Agazzi, Alessandro Bianco, Raffaella Brandoli, Miguel Barreiro, Mark Stanley, Frank Amankwah, Matteo Oriani, Manuele Mimo, Goy Oracha, Tommaso Magro, Sofia Faggian, Matteo Lanzi, Peter Elst, Francesca Beordo, Federico Pitone, Tiziano Fruet, Giorgio Pedergnani, Andrea Sgaravato, Fabio Bernardi, Sumi Lim, and many others.

Last but not least, I'd like to say thanks to my girlfriend and my life partner, Maela, for the amazing time we spend together; her passion and commitment in our relationship gives me the strength to go ahead and do my best everyday. Really, thanks, my love!

Jebin B V is a young frontend developer by profession and a full-stack developer. He has been into web development for the past 4 years and has a very good command over the design and development of commercial web applications. He also has a very good sense of design, interaction, and UX when it comes to web development.

Jebin has developed applications for real-time messaging, big data management, visualization, network shopping management, CMS, social networking, and so on. He has great interest in JavaScript, so anything that is from the JavaScript background excites him. He also has experience in PHP and Java.

He possesses a very good notion of application-level design when it comes to building frontend applications. He has the nonstop habit of learning on an everyday basis. He spends a great deal of time on updating himself with new things coming up in frontend technologies. He loves to learn, teach, master, and lead in his field of expertise.

www.PacktPub.com

Support files, eBooks, discount offers, and more

For support files and downloads related to your book, please visit www.PacktPub.com.

Did you know that Packt offers eBook versions of every book published, with PDF and ePub files available? You can upgrade to the eBook version at www.PacktPub.com and as a print book customer, you are entitled to a discount on the eBook copy. Get in touch with us at service@packtpub.com for more details.

At www.PacktPub.com, you can also read a collection of free technical articles, sign up for a range of free newsletters and receive exclusive discounts and offers on Packt books and eBooks.

https://www2.packtpub.com/books/subscription/packtlib

Do you need instant solutions to your IT questions? PacktLib is Packt's online digital book library. Here, you can search, access, and read Packt's entire library of books.

Why subscribe?

- Fully searchable across every book published by Packt
- Copy and paste, print, and bookmark content
- On demand and accessible via a web browser

Free access for Packt account holders

If you have an account with Packt at www.PacktPub.com, you can use this to access PacktLib today and view 9 entirely free books. Simply use your login credentials for immediate access.

Table of Contents

Preface

In this book, we will explore the concept and implementation of promises in JavaScript. This book has an evolving context that will lead you from a beginner's level to the master level of promises. Every chapter of this book will give you an outline to achieve a specific goal that will help you realize and quantify the amount of knowledge you absorb in every chapter.

The entire stack of chapters is designed in a way such that the book will evolve as you go through it. Every chapter in this book is designed in two parts: one is the concept building part and the other is the experimenting part, where you will be able to sample snippets of concepts, sometime in code, sometimes in best practices, and sometimes in images.

The first four chapters are more or less like theoretical knowledge to provide you with a solid foundation on JavaScript and promises. So, if you're a novice and don't know anything about JavaScript or promises, you will learn a great deal with these chapters. The rest of the chapters are more technology-oriented and you will learn implementation of promises in WinRT, Angular.js, jQuery, and Node.js. So, if you are a professional and already have some idea of promises, you may jump right into *Chapter 5, Promises in WinRT*, but I'd prefer it if you read through all the chapters for a better understanding of this book.

We will start with the introduction to JavaScript and how it has seen ups and downs from the late 90s up to the first decade of the twenty first century. We will focus on what asynchronous programing is and how JavaScript is using it. Moving on, I will introduce promises and its impact and how it's implemented. To make the book interesting and impart more knowledge to you, I will show you how promises has made its place in the heart of Java, one of the most mature object-oriented programming languages. This add-on content will act as a detour and clarify concepts in a more efficient way.

The flow of book will then lead you to the implementation of promises in some of the most used JavaScript libraries. We will see a sample code on how the mechanism of these libraries work. Finally, we will wrap up the book with our last chapter that will show you what is coming next in JavaScript, why it has gained so much attention over the past few years and what would be the possible future of JavaScript.

What this book covers

Chapter 1, Promises.js, covers the history of JavaScript and how it shaped into one of the leading technologies in modern application development. We will discuss why there was a need of JavaScript in the early 90s and how this language has seen ups and downs throughout its existence.

Chapter 2, The JavaScript Asynchronous Model, explains what a programming model is and how they are implemented in different languages, starting from a simple programming model to the synchronous model to the asynchronous model. We will also see how tasks are organized in memory and how they will serve according to their turns and priorities and how programming models decide what task is to be served.

Chapter 3, The Promise Paradigm, covers the paradigm of promise and the concept behind it. We will learn the conceptual knowledge of promise, deferred, common sequence of promise, and how promise helps in decoupling the business logic and application logic. We will also learn about the relationship between promises and event emitters and the concept behind the relation between promises and event emitters.

Chapter 4, Implementing Promises, discusses why we are implementing promises and why we chose Java as the core subject of this chapter. Java has richer features than any other programming language, and it also has better mechanism for asynchronous behavior. This chapter is the point where we start our journey to master promises.

Chapter 5, Promises in WinRT, explains how promises can be implemented in WinRT. We will see how promises evolved on the Windows platform and how it's contributing to different Windows-based devices.

Chapter 6, Promises in Node.js, covers what Node.js is, from where this most amazing library has evolved, who built it, and why and how it's helping us to create real-time web apps. We will see Q, the best way to offer promises to Node.js. We will see how we can work with Q, and then we will see different ways of using Q along with Node.js.

Chapter 7, Promises in Angular.js, explains how promises will be implemented in Angular.js, how it evolved and how promises will help in achieving applications composed for real-time web apps. We will also see the functionality of the Q library and the Angular.js implementation of promises using code and learn how to use them in our next application.

Chapter 8, Promises in jQuery, discusses how jQuery started taking shape and how it became a fundamental element of the modern-day web development. We will learn how to build basic jQuery documents and how to call the functions embedded into HTML files. We will learn why we started using deferred and promise in jQuery and how they are helping us to create cutting edge applications on both web-based platform and portable devices.

Chapter 9, JavaScript – The Future Is Now, covers how JavaScript is a game changer and how it has a bright future ahead. We will also explore why JavaScript has great tendency and adoptability, which will lead it to the next level of usage in almost every domain of computer science.

What you need for this book

If you are a software engineer who wants to learn more interesting facts about JavaScript to make your life easier, this book is for you. A simple and engaging language with narrations and code examples makes this book easy to understand and apply its practices. This book starts with an introduction to JavaScript promises and how it evolved over time. You will then learn the JavaScript asynchronous model and how JavaScript handles asynchronous programming. Next, you will learn about the promises paradigm and its advantages. Finally, this book will show you how to implement promises on platforms such as WinRT, jQuery, and Node.js, which are used in project development.

To get the best out of this book, you should know the basic programming concepts, the basic syntax of JavaScript, and possess a good understanding of HTML.

Who this book is for

This book is for all the software/web engineers who want to apply the promises paradigm in their next project and get the best outcome from it. This book has all the basic as well as advanced concepts of promises in JavaScript. This book can also act as a reference for the engineers who are already using promises in their projects and want to improve their current knowledge of this concept.

This book is a great resource for frontend engineers, but also serves as a learning guide for backend engineers who want to make sure their code collaborates seamlessly within the project.

Conventions

In this book, you will find a number of text styles that distinguish between different kinds of information. Here are some examples of these styles and an explanation of their meaning.

Code words in text, database table names, folder names, filenames, file extensions, pathnames, dummy URLs, user input, and Twitter handles are shown as follows: "The `click` function will call (or execute) the callback function we passed to it."

A block of code is set as follows:

```
Q.fcall(imException)
.then(
    // first handler-fulfill
    function() { },

);
```

Any command-line input or output is written as follows:

```
D:\> node -v
D:\> NPM  -v
```

New terms and **important words** are shown in bold. Words that you see on the screen, for example, in menus or dialog boxes, appear in the text like this: " It should turn into green and display the **Success** message."

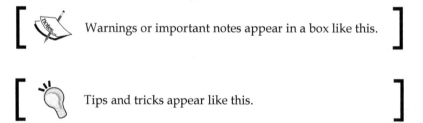

[![note] Warnings or important notes appear in a box like this.]

[![tip] Tips and tricks appear like this.]

Reader feedback

Feedback from our readers is always welcome. Let us know what you think about this book—what you liked or disliked. Reader feedback is important for us as it helps us develop titles that you will really get the most out of.

To send us general feedback, simply e-mail feedback@packtpub.com, and mention the book's title in the subject of your message.

If there is a topic that you have expertise in and you are interested in either writing or contributing to a book, see our author guide at www.packtpub.com/authors.

Customer support

Now that you are the proud owner of a Packt book, we have a number of things to help you to get the most from your purchase.

Downloading the example code

You can download the example code files from your account at http://www.packtpub.com for all the Packt Publishing books you have purchased. If you purchased this book elsewhere, you can visit http://www.packtpub.com/support and register to have the files e-mailed directly to you.

Errata

Although we have taken every care to ensure the accuracy of our content, mistakes do happen. If you find a mistake in one of our books—maybe a mistake in the text or the code—we would be grateful if you could report this to us. By doing so, you can save other readers from frustration and help us improve subsequent versions of this book. If you find any errata, please report them by visiting http://www.packtpub.com/submit-errata, selecting your book, clicking on the **Errata Submission Form** link, and entering the details of your errata. Once your errata are verified, your submission will be accepted and the errata will be uploaded to our website or added to any list of existing errata under the Errata section of that title.

To view the previously submitted errata, go to https://www.packtpub.com/books/content/support and enter the name of the book in the search field. The required information will appear under the **Errata** section.

Piracy

Piracy of copyrighted material on the Internet is an ongoing problem across all media. At Packt, we take the protection of our copyright and licenses very seriously. If you come across any illegal copies of our works in any form on the Internet, please provide us with the location address or website name immediately so that we can pursue a remedy.

Please contact us at `copyright@packtpub.com` with a link to the suspected pirated material.

We appreciate your help in protecting our authors and our ability to bring you valuable content.

Questions

If you have a problem with any aspect of this book, you can contact us at `questions@packtpub.com`, and we will do our best to address the problem.

1
Promises.js

In today's world, computer programming languages are getting much more advanced and there is a shift in the approach of using technologies. This is due to the fact that technology has been emerging with the rapid change in businesses and their needs. The vast expansion of business on electronic devices has led universities, researchers, and industries to invest in generating the latest technologies and tools that result in the inception of many new computer languages.

However, this is not the case with JavaScript. It's relatively new. It has been used and dumped at least three times by the modern programming landscape and is now widely accepted as the tool to develop modern, scalable, and real-time web applications in today's cyberspace.

In the mid 90s, the era of dot-com was born and it was during this time when companies wanted to dominate the newly created market called cyberspace. Although this was a virtual place and had no physical existence, the war for dominance was at its peak. Netscape Communications Corporation wanted its own variant of a lightweight interpreted language that would complement Java by appealing to nonprofessional programmers. This task was given to Brendan Eich who developed the first version of JavaScript with the name "Mocha". Officially, it was called LiveScript when it was first released in September 1995 in Netscape's browser in beta version 2.0.

However, the name was changed to JavaScript when the version 2.0 B3 rolled out later. Since 1995, JavaScript has seen many ups and downs. There are stories of it being adopted, rejected, and adopted again. Soon after its launch, JavaScript gained a very popular response throughout the industry. Every major company contributed to its growth and used it after slight adjustment for their needs.

The fall and rise of JavaScript

The Netscape browser witnessed the fall of JavaScript in the late 90s and early 2000. The face of web development was maturing, but very few were still interested in investing in JavaScript.

It was the advent of the Mozilla foundation that released the first open source browser, Firefox, in early 2002-2003 since the base was the successor of the former Netscape browser. They employed JavaScript again within their product. In 2004, Google introduced **Asynchronous JavaScript and XML (AJAX)**. This led to the foundation of many techniques and made communication easy with a black and white frontend and server by minimizing the server calls.

Google's contributions to JavaScript

Google has made more contributions in evolving, developing, and utilizing of JavaScript than any other organization. It was Google that introduced the V8 engine in its flagship web browser, Chrome. V8 is the backbone engine of the browser, and due to the smart usage of JavaScript, the browser is faster, robust, and adaptable to web and Android devices.

In the year 2009, Node.js arrived based on the same V8 engine as in Chrome. This is the server side of JavaScript, but far more better and advanced than what Netscape had introduced in late 90s. The whole idea of Node.js is to develop nonblocking **input/output (I/O)** and with few lines of codes, the server can serve up to 20K clients at a given slot of time.

Soon after Node.js, an entire stack of development has been introduced by the name of MEAN stack, which is an acronym of MongoDB, Express.js, Angular.js, and Node.js; where MongoDB is document based, NoSQL is a JavaScript-based database, Express. js is for a presentation layer, Angular.js is for frontend development of an app, and Node.js as the server that runs the entire show.

Where Promises.js came in?

Those of you who are aware of how a server-side script executes in an I/O event know that reading or writing data to and from a drive is blocking in nature, that is, during its execution, no other operation can be performed by a server-side language, even by the client. Well, with Promises.js, this is no longer the case. Promises.js utilizes a nonblocking strategy to perform I/O operations, so a client using your web app is free to perform any other tasks they want to without having to wait for the data read/write operation to be completed.

What is a promise?

When an eventual value is returned from the completion of a single operation, it represents a **promise**. If we analyze promise as a pact from human, it will help us understand the concept of promises in computer programming especially from the JavaScript perspective. Every promise is a pact among two or more parties to deliver some value to the other. The value can either be tangible or intangible, but a promise must deliver something in return. Until the promise is fulfilled, it remains in an unfulfilled state. However, when the said commitment has been made, the promise is said to be fulfilled. If the promise is not delivered as anticipated, the promise is said to fail.

So, what is a promise? According to the official definition:

> *Promise is an object or a function with a then method whose behavior confirms to this specification and represents the eventual result of an asynchronous operation.*

The source of this definition is slide number 21 at `http://www.slideshare.net/wookieb/callbacks-promises-generators-asynchronous-javascript`.

Why do we need promise in JS?

Promises.js is a JavaScript library that promises asynchronous I/O operations such as reading and writing on a file. Whenever there is a callback method that involves making all operations related to I/O, they are to be made asynchronous. This extra callback parameter confuses our idea of what is the input and what will be its return value. It never works with control flow primitives. It also doesn't handle errors thrown by a callback method.

So, we need to handle errors thrown by a callback method, but also need to be careful not to handle errors thrown by the callback method. By the time we are done with this, our code will be a mess of error handling.

Despite all this mess of error handling code, we are still left with the problem of the extra callback parameter hanging around. Promises help you naturally handle errors, and write cleaner code by not having callback parameters.

Software prerequisites

Before starting *Chapter 2*, The *JavaScript Asynchronous Model*, you must need a set of prerequisite concepts that will make you better understand where to use Promises.js, and how it can save your time and effort in your recent or upcoming projects. The following section will elaborate what these concepts are and how we will use these as a base for our understanding of promise.

The prerequisite of this book is that you have a good understanding of procedural programing and a compulsory knowledge of basic JavaScript. Since this book is designed to develop a deeper knowledge of a concept (promise) and its use in different technologies, it's also imperative that you have a very good understanding of HTML and how to embed the code for your need.

An understanding of basic programming will help you begin with experiments with the help of a sample code as soon as you are done with any chapter/section. In this book, I've tried to make every section self-explanatory and every sample of code as a standalone script/program up to maximum strength. However, where there was need, we've added a snippet of code or algorithm to present our point more clearly.

Environment you need before getting started

To use the code within this book, you don't need any extra piece of software/IDE to start. To sample the code provided in this book, you only need free software/IDE such as Notepad++ or any other preferred open source GPL or GNU product.

Also, to view the result of your code, you need a web browser such as Google's Chrome or Mozilla's Firefox. For some examples related to Microsoft technologies, you will need Internet Explorer 9 or higher.

Future, promise, and delay

Future, promise, and delay describe an object that acts as proxy to a result that is initially unknown due to computation of its value, which is yet to be completed. They are normally referred to as constructs used for synchronizing in some concurrent programming language.

Daniel P. Friedman and David Wise proposed the term "promise" in 1975. Peter Hibbard called it "eventual". The term promise was coined by Liskov and Shrira, although they referred to the pipelining mechanism by the name "call-stream". The term promise refers to the fact that in completion of any said operation, an eventual value will be obtained. In the same way, the value can also be taken as eventual because it will only yield out on the occurrence of any event. Thus, both terms refer to the same fact simultaneously.

The terms future, promise, and delay are often used interchangeably. There is some core difference in implementing these terms. Future is revered as the read-only placeholder view of the variable, while promise is a writeable single assignment container that sets the value of the future.

In many cases, future promise are created together. In simple words, future is a value and promise is a function that sets the value. The future reruns the value of an async function (promise); setting the value of future is also called **resolving**, **fulfilling**, or **binding** it.

Promise pipelining

Using future can dramatically reduce the latency in distributed systems; for example, promise enables promise pipelining in programming languages E and Joule, which were also called **call-stream** in the Argus language.

A note to remember here is that promise pipelining should be distinguished from a parallel asynchronous message passing to a system supporting parallel message passing but not pipelining. It should also not be confused with pipelined message processing in actor systems, where it is possible for an actor to specify and begin executing a behavior for the next message before having completed processing of the current message.

Read-only views

The read-only view allows reading its value when resolved, but doesn't permit you to resolve it, thus making it possible to obtain a read-only view of the future.

The support for read-only views is consistent with the principle of least authority.

The read-only view enables you to set the value to be restricted to the subject that needs to set it. The sender of an asynchronous message (with result) receives the read-only promise for the result, and the target of the message receives the resolver.

States of a promise

Promise is based on three states. Each state has a significance and can be used to drive a certain level of result as per the need. This can help a programmer choose as per his/her need. The three states of a promise are as follows:

- **Pending**: This is the initial state of a promise
- **Fulfilled**: This is the state of a promise representing a successful operation
- **Rejected**: This is the state of a promise representing a failed operation

Once a promise is fulfilled or rejected, it is immutable (that is, it can never change again).

With reference to the concepts discussed earlier, it's now clear what a promise is and how you can use it with all its potential.

How do we keep Promises.js in this book?

This book will cover the use of Promises.js with every major technology that has implemented the concept of promise. The book has been carefully divided into chapters to introduce, discuss, and explain the use of promise within that particular technology. Every chapter has its standalone set of examples of code to better understand the best use of Promises.js and its outcome.

The examples will be assuming that the selection of an operating system is purely your discretion. It may vary from reader to reader based on his/her licenses.

All the code is clearly printed with instructions and comments for a better understanding. Also, a soft copy is provided with this book enlisting every piece of code sorted in its respective chapter/section.

Browser compatibility

Promises support is extended to many modern browsers but not to all. A handy reference of what browser it supports is given in desktop and mobile screen resolutions:

- Desktop compatibility:

Feature	Chrome	Firefox	Internet Explorer	Opera	Safari
Basic support	36	31	Not supported till IE 11. Added in Edge	27	8

- Mobile compatibility:

Feature	Android	Firefox Mobile (Gecko)	IE Mobile	Opera Mobile	Safari Mobile	Chrome for Android
Basic support	4.4.4	31	Edge	Not supported	Not supported	42

Summary

In this chapter, we learned where JavaScript began and how it shaped into one of the leading technologies in modern application development. We discussed why there was a need for JavaScript in the early 90s and how this language has seen ups and downs throughout its existence.

We have also seen how investments from tech companies made their contributions in creating, developing, and evolving JavaScript as a major player in a dynamic and fast growing market of web, mobile, and real-time apps.

The adaptation of promises concept will make JavaScript much stronger and will help developers and engineers to write better code in an efficient manner.

In the next chapter, we will see what is an asynchronous model and how it's better fitted with JavaScript. This will help us understand to adopt and implement Promises.js in various languages.

2
The JavaScript Asynchronous Model

In this chapter, we will look at the model behind asynchronous programming, why it was needed, and how it is implemented in JavaScript.

We will also learn what a programming model is and its significance, starting from a simple programming model to a synchronous model to an asynchronous model. Since our prime focus is on JavaScript, which employs an asynchronous programming model, we will discuss it in more detail than the rest of the models.

Let's start with what models are and their significance.

Models are basically templates upon which the logics are designed and fabricated within a compiler/interpreter of a programming language so that software engineers can use these logics in writing their software logically. Every programming language we use is designed on a particular programming model. Since software engineers are asked to solve a particular problem or to automate any particular service, they adopt programming languages as per the need.

There is no set rule that assigns a particular language to create products. Engineers adopt any language based on the need.

Programming models

Ideally, we will focus on three major programming models, which are as follows:

- The first one is a single-threaded synchronous model
- The second one a is multithreaded model
- The third one is an asynchronous programming model

Since JavaScript employs an asynchronous model, we will discuss it in greater detail. However, let's start by explaining what these programming models are and how they facilitate their end users.

The single-threaded synchronous model

The single-threaded synchronous model is a simple programming model or single-threaded synchronous programming model, in which one task follows the other. If there is a queue of tasks, the first task is given first priority, and so on and so forth. It's the simplest way of getting things done, as shown in the following diagram:

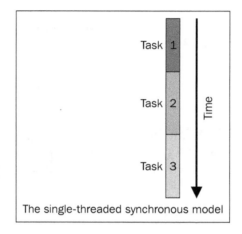

The single-threaded synchronous model

The single-threaded synchronous programming model is one of the best examples of a Queue data structure, which follows the **First In First Out (FIFO)** rule. This model assumes that if **Task 2** is being executed at the moment, it must have been done after **Task 1** was finished without errors with all the output available as predicted or needed. This programming model is still supported for writing down simple programs for simple devices.

The multithreaded synchronous model

Unlike single-thread programming, in multi-thread programming, every task is performed in a separate thread, so multiple tasks need multiple threads. The threads are managed by the operating system, and may run concurrently on a system with multiple process or multiple cores.

It seems quite simple that multiple threads are managed by the OS or the program in which it's being executed; it's a complex and time-consuming task that requires multiple level of communications between the threads in order to conclude the task without any deadlock and errors, as can be seen from the following diagram:

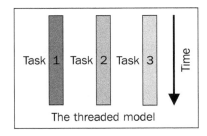

The threaded model

Some programs implement parallelism using multiple processes instead of multiple threads, although the programming details are different.

The asynchronous programming model

Within the asynchronous programming model, tasks are interleaved with one another in a single thread of control.

This single thread may have multiple embedded threads and each thread may contain several tasks linked up one after another. This model is simpler in comparison to the threaded case, as the programmers always know the priority of the task executing at a given slot of time in memory.

Consider a task in which an OS (or an application within OS) uses some sort of a scenario to decide how much time is to be allotted to a task, before giving the same chance to others. The behavior of the OS of taking control from one task and passing it on to another task is called **preempting**.

 The multithreaded sync model is also referred to as **preemptive multitasking**. When it's asynchronous, it's called **cooperative multitasking**.

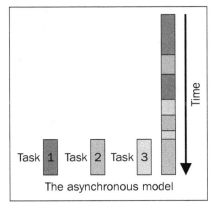

The asynchronous model

With threaded systems, the priority to suspend one thread and put another on the exaction is not in the programmer's hand; it's the base program that controls it. In general, it's controlled by the operating system itself, but this is not the case with an asynchronous system.

In asynchronous systems, the control of execution and suspension of a thread is in complete discretion of the programmer and the thread won't change its state until it's explicitly asked to do so.

Densities with an asynchronous programming model

With all these qualities of an asynchronous programming model, it has its densities to deal with.

Since the control of execution and priority assignment is in a programmer's hand, he/she will have to organize each task as a sequence of smaller steps that are executed immediately. If one task uses the output of the other, the dependent task must be engineered so that it can accept its input as a sequence of bits not together; this is how programmers fabricate their tasks on and set their priorities. The soul of an asynchronous system that can outperform synchronous systems almost dramatically is when the tasks are forced to wait or are blocked.

Why do we need to block the task?

A more common reason why a task is forcefully blocked is that it is waiting to perform an I/O or transfer data to and from an external device. A normal CPU can handle data transfer faster than any network link is capable of, which in result makes a synchronous program blocked that is spending so much time on I/O. Such programs are also referred as **blocking programs** for this reason.

The whole idea behind an asynchronous model is avoid wasting CPU time and avoid blocking bits. When an asynchronous program encounters a task that will normally get blocked in a synchronous program, it will instead execute some other tasks that can still make progress. Because of this, asynchronous programs are also called **non-blocking program**.

Since the asynchronous program spends less time waiting and roughly giving an equal amount of time to every task, it supersedes synchronous programs.

Compared to the synchronous model, the asynchronous model performs best in the following scenarios:

- There are a large number of tasks, so it's likely that there is always at least one task that can make progress

- The tasks perform lots of I/O, causing a synchronous program to waste lots of time blocking, when other tasks are running

- The tasks are largely independent from one another, so there is little need for intertask communication (and thus for one task to wait for another)

Keeping all the preceding points in mind, it will almost perfectly highlight a typical busy network, say a web server in a client-server environment, where each task represents a client requesting some information from the server. In such cases, an asynchronous model will not only increase the overall response time, but also add value to the performance by serving more clients (requests) at a time.

Why not use some more threads?

At this point, you may ask why not add another thread by not relying on a single thread. Well, the answer is quite simple. The more the threads, the more memory it will consume, which in turn will create low performance and a higher turnaround time. Using more threads doesn't only come with a cost of memory, but also with effects on performance. With each thread, a certain overhead is linked to maintain the state of that particular thread, but multiple threads will be used when there is an absolute need of them, not for each and every other thing.

Learning the JavaScript asynchronous model

Keeping this knowledge in mind, if we see what the JavaScript asynchronous model is, we can now clearly relate to an asynchronous model in JavaScript and understand how it's implemented.

In non-web languages, most of the code we write is synchronous, that is, blocking. JavaScript does its stuff in a different way.

JavaScript is a single-threaded language. We already know what single threaded actually means for the sake of simplicity – two bits of the same script cannot run at the same time. In browsers, JavaScript shares a thread with loads of other processes inline. These "inline processes" can be different from one browser to another, but typically, **JavaScript (JS)** is in the same queue as painting, updating styles, and handling user actions (an activity in one of these processes delays the others).

As in the image beneath, whenever the asynchronous (non-blocking) script executes in a browser, it goes from top to bottom in an execution pattern. Starting from the page load, the script goes to a document object where the JavaScript object is created. The script then goes into the parsing phase where all the nodes and HTML tags are added. After the completion of parsing, the whole script will be loaded in the memory as an asynchronous (non-blocking) script.

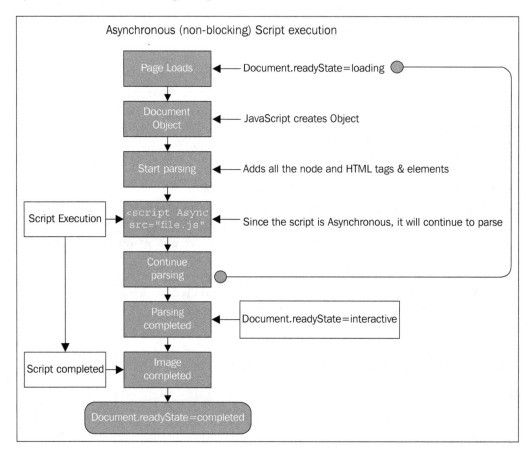

How JavaScript implements an asynchronous model

JavaScript uses an loop event and its cycle is called a "tick" (as in a clock), since it runs within the time slot bound by the CPU. An interpreter is responsible for checking whether every tick is an asynchronous callback to be executed. All other synchronous operations take place within the same tick. The time value passed is not guaranteed — there's no way of knowing how long it will take until the next tick, so we usually say the callbacks will run "as soon as possible"; although, some calls may even be dropped.

> An **interpreter** is the translator program built into the browsers that translates the entire code to a human-readable language. As it reads line by line, if there is any error in any line, it will stop execution and present the error on the page.

Within JavaScript, there are four core ways on how an asynchronous model is implemented in it. These four methods help not only for better performance of your program, but also in easier maintainability of code. These four methods are as follows:

- A callback function
- The event listener
- The publisher/subscriber
- The promises object

Callbacks in JavaScript

In JavaScript, functions are first class citizens, which means they can be treated as objects and because of the fact that they really are objects themselves. They can do what a regular object is capable of, such as these:

- Stored in variables
- Passed as augments to other functions
- Created within functions
- Returned from functions after a payload of some processed data mechanism

A callback function, also known as a higher-order function, is a function that is passed to another function (let's call this other function as otherFunction) as a parameter, and the callback function is called (executed) inside otherFunction.

A callback function is essentially a pattern (an established solution to a common problem), and therefore the use of a callback function is also known as a callback pattern. Because functions are first class objects, we can use callback functions in JavaScript.

Since functions are first class objects, we can use callback functions in JavaScript, but what are callback functions? The idea behind callback functions is derived from functional programming, which uses functions as arguments as implementing callback functions is as easy as passing regular variables as arguments to functions.

A common use of a callback function can be seen in the following lines of code:

```
$("#btn_1).click().click.function() {
alert ("Button one was clicked");
});
```

The code explains itself as follows:

- We pass a function as a parameter to the `click` function
- The `click` function will call (or execute) the callback function we passed to it

This is a typical use of callback functions in JavaScript, and indeed, it is widely used in jQuery. We will examine promise with respect to jQuery in more details in *Chapter 8, Promises in jQuery*.

Blocking functions

While we are discussing what a blocking function in JavaScript is and how one should implement it, many of us really don't clearly understand what we mean by a blocking function in JavaScript.

As humans, we have a mind that is designed in such a way that it can do many tasks at a time, such as while reading this book, you are aware of the surroundings around you, you can think and type simultaneously, and you can talk to someone while you are driving.

These examples are for multithreaded models, but is there any blocking function in our human body? The answer is yes. We have a blocking function because of which we all have other activities in our mind and within our body; it stops for a tiny pinch of a nanosecond. This blocking function is called sneezing. When any human sneezes, all the functions related to mind and body became blocked for a tiny fraction of nanosecond. This is rarely noticed by people. The same goes with the blocking function of JavaScript.

The mechanism of a callback function in JavaScript

The question here is, how on earth does a callback function work?

As we know that functions are like first class objects in JS, we can pass them around in a similar way to variables and return them as functions and use them in other functions.

When we pass a callback function as arguments to another function, we are only passing the function definition. We aren't executing functions in parameters. We are also not passing the function with the trailing pair of executing parenthesis (), as we would when we are executing a function.

Since the containing function has the callback function in its parameter as a function definition, it can execute the callback at any time.

It is important to note that the callback function is not executed immediately. It is "called back" and can still be accessed later via the arguments object by the containing function.

Basic rules to implement callbacks

There are some basic rules that you need to keep in mind while you are implementing the callbacks.

Callbacks are normally simple, but you should be familiar with the rule if you are crafting your own callback functions. Here are some key pointers that you must take into account while you are working on your callback functions:

- Use named or anonymous functions as callbacks
- Pass parameters to callback functions
- Make sure callback is a function before executing it

Handling callback hell

As JavaScript uses callback functions to handle asynchronous control flow, working with nesting of callbacks can become messy and most of the time, out of control.

One needs to be very careful while writing callbacks or using it from any other library.

Here is what happens if the callbacks are not handled properly:

```
func1(param, function (err, res)) {
    func1(param, function (err, res)) {
        func1(param, function (err, res)) {
            func1(param, function (err, res)) {
                func1(param, function (err, res)) {
                    func1(param, function (err, res)) {
                        //do something
                    });
                });
            });
        });
    });
});
```

The preceding situation is commonly referred to as **callback hell**. This is quite common in JavaScript, which makes the lives of engineers miserable. This also makes the code hard for other team members to understand and hard to maintain for further use. The most drastic of all is that it confuses an engineer, making it hard for him/her to remember where to pass on the control.

Here are the quick reminders for callback hell:

- Never let your function be unnamed. Give your function an understandable and meaningful name. The name must show it's a callback function that is performing certain operations instead of defining an anonymous function in the parameter of the main function.

- Make your code less scary to look at and easier to edit, refactor, and hack on later. Most of the engineers write code in a flow of thought with less focus on beautification of code, which makes it difficult to maintain the code later. Use online tools such as `http://www.jspretty.com` to add readability to your code.

- Separate your code into modules; don't write all your logic in a single module. Instead, write short meaningful modules so that you can export a section of code that does a particular job. You can then import that module into your larger application. This approach can also help you reuse the code in similar applications, thus making a whole library of your modules.

The events

Events are signals that are generated when a specific action takes place. JavaScript
is aware of such signals and responds accordingly.

Events are messages fired in a constant stream as the user works along. Events are
normally based on user actions, and if programmed well, they act upon as directed.
Any event is useless if it doesn't have a handler that works to handle events.

Since JavaScript provides a handsome control to programmers/engineers, it's their
ability to handle events, monitor, and respond to them. The more capable you are at
handling events, the more interactive your application will be.

The mechanism of event handling

There are two conventional ways to implement events in JavaScript. The first one
is via HTML using attributes and second is via script.

To make your application respond to a user's action, you need to do the following:

1. Decide which event should be monitored.
2. Set up event handlers that trigger functions when an event occurs.
3. Write the functions that provide the appropriate responses to the events.

The event handler is always the name of the event perceived by on, for example,
click event handled by a event handler, onClick(). This event handler causes a
function to run, and the function provides the response to the event.

DOM – event capture and event bubbling

Document Object Model (DOM) makes it much easier to detect the events and assign related event handlers to react to them. This uses two concepts of event capture and event bubbling for this purpose. Let's take a look at how each can help in detecting and assigning the right handler for the right event.

Capturing an event is referred to as the process of an event as it commutes to its destination document. Also, it has the ability to capture or intercept this event.

This makes the whole round trip go incrementally downwards to its containing elements of the tree until it reaches to itself.

On the contrary, event bubbling is the inverse of event capture. With bubbling, the event is first captured and handled by the innermost element and then propagated to the outer elements.

A list of the most common events handlers

There is an entire array of event handlers to be put to use for different needs and situations, but let's add a few more common and regular events handlers.

 Please bear in mind that some event handlers may vary from one browser to another, and this specification becomes more limited when it comes to Microsoft's Internet Explorer or Mac's Safari.

The following list is quite handy and self-explanatory. To use this list more effectively, I recommend developers/engineers to make a handy note of it for reference.

Event category	When will the event be triggered	Event handler
Browser events	A page completes loading	Onload
	The page is removed from the browser window	Onunload
	JavaScript throws an error	Onerror
Mouse events	The user clicks over an element	onclick
	The user double-clicks over an element	ondblclick
	The mouse button is pressed down over an element	onmousedown
	The mouse button is released over an element	onmouseup
	The mouse pointer moves onto an element	onmouseover
	The mouse pointer leaves an element	Onmouseout

Event category	When will the event be triggered	Event handler
Keyboard events	A key is pressed	onkeydown
	A key is released	onkeyup
	A key is pressed and released	Onkeypress
Form events	The element receives focus from a pointer or by tabbing navigation	onfocus
	The element loses focus	onblur
	The user selects the type in text or text area field	onselect
	The user submits a form	onsubmit
	The user resets a form	onreset
	The field loses focus and the content has changed since receiving focus	onchange

As mentioned earlier, these are the most common list of event handlers. There is a separate list of specifications for Microsoft's Internet explorer that can be found at `http://msdn.microsoft.com/en-us/library/ie/ms533051(v=vs.85).aspx`.

A complete list of the event's compatibility can be seen at:

`http://www.quirksmode.org/dom/events/index.html`

Triggering functions in response to events

JavaScript events need triggering in order to get a response. An event handler is responsible for responding to such events, but there are four commonly used ways to trigger events in a proper manner:

- The JavaScript pseudo protocol
- The inline event handler
- The handler as an object property
- Event listeners

Types of events in JavaScript

There are many different types of events in JavaScript, some listed as follows:

- Interface events
- Mouse events
- Form events

- W3C events
- Microsoft events
- Mozilla events

Interface events

The interface events occur due to the user's action. When the user clicks on any element, he/she always causes a click event. When clicking on the element has specific purpose, an additional interface event is caused.

Mouse events

When the user moves the mouse into the link area, the mouseover event fires. When he/she clicks on it, the click event fires.

Form events

Forms recognize submit and reset events, which predictably, fire when the user submits or resets a form. The submit event is the key of any form of a validation script.

W3C events

W3C events fire when the DOM structure of a document is changed. The most general one is the `DOMSubtreeModified` event that is fired when the DOM tree below the HTML element is triggered.

The DOM 2 event specification can be seen at `http://www.w3.org/TR/2000/REC-DOM-Level-2-Events-20001113/events.html#Events-eventgroupings-mutationevents`.

Microsoft events

Microsoft has created a number of its own event's handler specification, which (of course) can only run on its platform. This can be seen at `http://msdn.microsoft.com/en-us/library/ie/ms533051(v=vs.85).aspx`.

Mozilla events

Mozilla has its own specification, and it be seen at `https://developer.mozilla.org/en/docs/Web/API/Event`.

The publisher/subscriber

Events are yet another solution to communicate when asynchronous callbacks finish execution. An object can become emitter and publish events that other objects can listen to. This is one of the finest examples of the observer pattern.

The nature of this method is similar to "event listener", but much better than the latter because we can view the "message center" in order to find out how much signal is present and the number of subscribers for each signal, which runs the monitoring program.

A brief account of the observer pattern

The observer provides very loose coupling between objects. This provides the ability to broadcast changes to those who are listening to it. This broadcast may be for the single observer or a group of observers who are waiting to listen. The subject maintains a list of observers to whom it has to broadcast the updates. The subject also provides an interface for objects to register themselves. If they are not in the list, the subject doesn't care who or what is listening to it. This is the way how the subject is decoupled from the observers, allowing easy replacement of one observer for another observer or even one subject, as long as it maintains the same series of events.

A formal definition of observer

The following is the definition of observer:

> *Define a one-to-many dependency between objects so that when one object changes state, all its dependents are notified and updated automatically.*

> *– Gang of Four*

The source of this definition is page 20 of *Design Patterns: Elements of Reusable Object-Oriented Software*, Addison-Wesley Professional.

The push and pull model

When you create a subject/observer relationship, you would want to send information to the subject; sometimes, this information can be brief, or sometimes, it can be additional information. This can also happen that your observer sends a little chunk of information, and in return, your subject queries more information in response.

When you're sending a lot of information, it's referred to as the **push** model, and when the observers query for more information, it's referred to as the **pull** model.

The pull model emphasizes the subject's ignorance of its observers, whereas the push model assumes subjects know something about their observers' needs. The push model might make observers less reusable because Subject classes make assumptions about Observer classes that might not always be true. On the other hand, the pull model may be inefficient because Observer classes must ascertain what changed without help from the Subject.

— Gang of Four

The source of this definition is page 320, *Design Patterns: Elements of Reusable Object-Oriented Software, Addison-Wesley Professional.*

The advent of observer/push-pub

This observer/push-pub pattern provides a way of thinking on how to maintain relationship between different parts of an application. This also gives us an idea of what part of our application should be replaced with observers and subjects in order to achieve maximum performance and maintainability. Here are some points to bear in mind when using this pattern in JavaScript in particular, and for other languages in general:

- Using this pattern, it can break down an application into smaller, more loosely coupled blocks to improve code management and potential for reuse
- The observer pattern is best when there is a need to maintain consistency between related objects, without making classes tightly coupled
- Due to the dynamic relationship that exists between observers and subjects, it provides great flexibility, which may not be as easy to implement when disparate parts of our application are tightly coupled

The drawbacks of observer/push-pub

Since every pattern has its own price, it is the same with this pattern. The most common one is due to its loosely coupled nature, it's sometimes hard to maintain the states of objects and track the path of information flow, resulting in getting irrelevant information to subjects by those who have not subscribed for this information.

The more common drawbacks are as follows:

- By decoupling publishers from subscribers, it can sometimes become difficult to obtain guarantees that particular parts of our application are functioning as we may expect
- Another drawback of this pattern is that subscribers are unaware of the existence of each other and are blind to the cost of switching between publishers
- Due to the dynamic relationship between subscribers and publishers, the update dependency can be difficult to track

The promises object

The promises object is the last of the major concepts of asynchronous programming model implemented. We will be looking at promise as a design pattern.

Promise is a relatively new concept in JavaScript, but it's been around for a long time and has been implemented in other languages.

Promise is an abstraction that contains two main properties, which make them easier to work with:

- You can attach more than one callback with a single promise
- Values and states (errors) get passed along
- Due to these properties, a promise makes common asynchronous patterns using callback easy

A promise can be defined as:

> *A promise is an observable token given from one object to another. Promises wrap an operation and notify their observers when the operation either succeeds or fails.*

The source of this definition is *Design Patterns: Elements of Reusable Object-Oriented Software, Addison-Wesley Professional.*

Since the scope of this book revolves around the promise and how it is implemented, we will discuss it in greater detail in *Chapter 3, The Promise Paradigm.*

Summing up – the asynchronous programing model

So far, we have seen how the asynchronous model is implemented in JavaScript. This is one core aspect of understanding that JavaScript has its own implementation for the asynchronous programming model, and it has employed much of the core concepts in the asynchronous programming model.

- The asynchronous mode is very important. In the browser, a very time-consuming operation should be performed asynchronously, avoiding the browser unresponsive time; the best example is the Ajax operations.
- On the server side, the asynchronous mode of execution since the environment is single threaded. So, if you allow synchronization to perform all http requests, server performance will decline sharply and will soon lose responsiveness.
- These are simple reasons why implementation on JavaScript is widely accepted in modern applications on all ends of needs. Databases such as MongoDB, Node.js as Server Side JavaScript, Angular.js, and Express.js as frontend, and logic building tools are examples of how heavily JavaScript is implemented throughout the industry. Their stack is commonly refer red to as the MEAN stack (MongoDB, Angular.js, Express.js, and Node.js)

Summary

In this chapter, we learned what a programming model is and how they are implemented in different languages, starting from a simple programming model to the synchronous model to the asynchronous model.

We also saw how tasks were organized in the memory and how they were served according to their turns and priorities, and how programming models decide what task is to be served.

We have also seen how the asynchronous programming model works in JavaScript, and why it's necessary to learn the dynamics of the asynchronous model to write better, maintainable, and robust code.

This chapter also explained how the major concepts of JavaScript are implemented and their roles from different angles in an application development.

We have also seen how callbacks, events, and observer were applied within JavaScript and how these core concepts are driving today's application development scenes.

In the next chapter, *Chapter 3, The Promise Paradigm*, we will learn a great deal about promise and how it's helping in making applications more robust and scalable.

3
The Promise Paradigm

In this chapter, we will focus on what the promises paradigm is, from where it originated, how languages implement it, and what problems it can solve for us.

We have briefly discussed the origin of the promise pattern in *Chapter 1, Promises.js*. In this chapter, we will explore this subject in more detail, in a generic way, so that it would clear the logic and theory behind the adoption of promise in different languages and in particular, how it's helping us in today's modern programming.

Callback, revisited

In previous chapters, you learned how the JavaScript mechanism works. The single-threaded model of JavaScript has its limitation, which can be controlled through better use of callbacks. However, the scenarios such as callback hell really pushed engineers to find and implement a better way to control the callbacks and maximize the performance of the program, while staying inside a single thread. A callback is a function that can be passed as an argument to another function to be executed when it's called.

There is absolutely no harm in using callbacks, but there are also a number of other options available to handle asynchronous events. Promise is one such way to handle asynchronous events and has more efficiency than many of other asynchronous tools in its family.

To understand more clearly why we needed to implement Promises.js in asynchronous programming, we need to understand the concept behind the promise and deferred objects.

Promise

The beauty of working with JavaScript's asynchronous events is that the program continues its execution, even when it doesn't have any value it needs to work that is in progress. Such scenarios are named as yet known values from unfinished work. This can make working with asynchronous events in JavaScript challenging.

Promises are a programming construct that represents a value that is still unknown. Promises in JavaScript enable us to write asynchronous code in a parallel manner to synchronous code.

Deferred

Deferred is an object that represents work that is not yet being done, and promise is an object representing a value that is not yet known.

The objects provide a way to take care of registering multiple callbacks into a self-managed callbacks queues, invoke callbacks queues, and relay the success or failure state of any synchronous function.

How do promise and deferred relate to each other?

So far, in *Chapter 2, The JavaScript Asynchronous Model*, we discussed promises and how they work. Let's have a look at how promises and deferred work:

1. Every deferred object has a promise that serves as a proxy for the future result.

2. A deferred object can be resolved or rejected by its caller, which separates the promise from the resolver, while a promise is a value returned by an asynchronous function.

3. The promise can be given to a number of consumers and each will observe the resolution incessantly, while the resolver/deferred can be given to any number of users and the promise will be resolved by the one that first resolved it.

Standard behaviors of the Promise API

There are few standards as per a promise/proposal, which has to be fulfilled for the true implementation of the concept. These standards are the keys to implement promises, and any library/language must comply with it for true implementation.

A promise does the following:

- A promise returns an eventual value when a single completion of an operation occurs.

- A promise has three states: unfulfilled (when a promise is waiting to be processed), fulfilled (when a promise has been completed and the desired result has been obtained), and finally, failed (when the result of a promise was obtained but not as anticipated).

- Promise has a `then` property, which must be a function and must return a promise. In order to complete a promise, `fulfilledHandler`, `errorHandler`, and `progressHandler` must be called in.

- With a promise, callback handlers return the fulfillment value from the returned promise.

- The promise value must be persistent. This should maintain a state, and within that state, the value must be preserved.

This API does not define how promises are created. It only provides a necessary interface that promise provides to promise consumers to interact with it. Implementations are free to define how promises are generated. Some promise may provide their own function to fulfill the promise and other promises may be fulfilled by mechanisms that are not visible to the promise consumer. Promises themselves may include other additional convenient methods as well.

Interactive promises

Interactive promises are extended promises that add more value to the paradigm by adding two more functions to its arsenal, `get` and `call`:

- `get(propertyName)`: This function requests the given property from the target of promise. This also returns a promise to provide the value of the stated property from promise's target.

- `call(functionName, arg1, arg2...)`: This function requests to call the given method/function on the target of promise. It also returns a promise to provide the return value of the requested function call.

The states and return values of a promise

From *Chapter 1, Promises.js*, we are already aware that a promise is based on three states. Let's brush up our memory on these states, in accordance with promises paradigm.

Promise has three states:

- Unfulfilled promise
- Fulfilled promise
- Failed promise

A promise exists within these three states.

The beginning of a promise is from an unfulfilled state. This is due to the fact that a promise is a proxy for an unknown value.

When the promise is filled with the value it's waiting for, it's in the fulfilled state. The promise will be labeled as failed if it returns an exception.

A promise may move from an unfulfilled to a fulfilled or failed state. Observers (or the objects/events waiting) are notified when the promise is either rejected or fulfilled. Once the promise is rejected or resolved, its output (value or state) cannot be modified.

The following code snippet will help you understand more easily than theory:

```
// Promise to be filled with future value
var futureValue = new Promise();

// .then() will return a new promise
var anotherFutureValue = futureValue.then();

// Promise state handlers (must be a function ).
// The returned value of the fulfilled / failed handler will be the
value of the promise.
futureValue.then({

    // Called if/when the promise is fulfilled
    fulfilledHandler: function() {},

    // Called if/when the promise fails
    errorHandler: function() {},

    // Called for progress events (not all implementations of promises
have this)
    progressHandler: function() {}
});
```

Common sequencing patterns

Promise and deferred enables us to represent simple tasks combined with complex tasks to a fine-grained control over their sequences.

As mentioned earlier, deferred is an object that represents work that is not being done yet and promise is an object representing a value that is currently unknown. This concept helps us write asynchronous JavaScript, similar to how we write synchronous code.

Promises make it comparatively easy to abstract small pieces of functionality shared across multiple asynchronous tasks. Let's take a look at the most common sequencing patterns that promises makes easier:

- Stacked
- Parallel
- Sequential

Stacked

Stacked binds multiple handlers anywhere in the application to the same promise event. This helps us bind a number of handlers in a cleaner way so that it gives control to sequence within our code. Here is a sample for stacked and bind handlers:

```
var req = $.ajax(url);
  req.done(function () {
      console.log('your assigned Request has been completed');
  });

  //Somewhere in the application
  req.done(function (retrievedData) {
      $('#contentPlaceholder').html(retrievedData);
  });
```

Parallel

Parallel simply asks multiple promises to return a single promise, which alerts of their multiple completion.

With the parallel sequence, you can write multiple promises to return a single promise. In a parallel sequence, an array of asynchronous tasks are executed concurrently and return a single promise when all the tasks have succeeded or rejected with an error in case of failure.

A general code snippet that shows how parallel sequence returns a single promise is shown as follows:

```
$.when(task01, task02).done(function () {
        console.log('taskOne and taskTwo were finished');
});
```

For a more clear understanding, here is a sample function that processes the parallel sequence:

```
function testPromiseParallelSequence(tasks)
{

    var results = [];   //an array of async tasks

    //tasks.map() will map all the return call was made.

    taskPromises = tasks.map(function(task)
    {
        return task();
    }); //returning all the promise
```

Sequential

Actions need to be in sequence if the output of one action is an input to another. HTTP requests are such a case where one action is an input to the other. Sequence also enables you to transfer the control of one part of the code to the other.

It executes tasks in a sequential order that is defined by the need of the application, or the scope of the tasks that need to be queued in order to be served.

Here is a generic example in which one sequence processes and passes control to the other as an input:

```
// seq1 and seq2 represents sequence one and two respectively
var seq1, seq2, url;
url = 'http://sampleurl.com;
seq1 = $.ajax(url);
    seq2 = seq1.then(

    function (data) {
        var def = new $.Deferred();

        setTimeout(function () {
```

```
            console.log('Request completed');
            def.resolve();
        },1000);

    return def.promise();
},

  function (err) {
      console.log('sequence 1 failed: Ajax request');
  }
);
seq2.done(function () {
    console.log('Sequence completed')
    setTimeout("console.log('end')",500);
});
```

Decoupling events and applications logic

Promises provide an efficient way to decouple the events and application logic.
This makes the implementation of events and application logic easier to build and
maintenance also saleable.

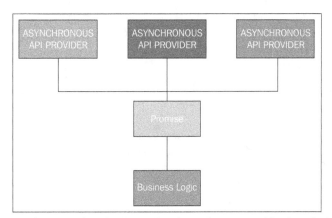

A simple way to show how promises decouple events and business logic

The significance of durability in promises is that it's not an "EventEmitter", but can
be converted into one by intelligent implementation. But then again, it would be a
crippled one.

Promises as event emitters

The problem in using promises as an event emitter is it's composition. It's the progression events in promises that cannot compose very well with EventEmitter. Promises chain and compose whereas events, on the other hand, are unable to do so. An implementation of Q library is discarding the progression in favor of estimation in v2. This is why progression was never included in ECMAScript 6. We will learn a great deal about a few of these emerging technologies in *Chapter 9, JavaScript – The Future Is Now*.

Coming back to our topic of how promises is decoupling events and applications logic, we can use events to trigger the resolution/failure of promises by passing the value at the same time, which allows us to decouple. Here is the code:

```
var def, getData, updateUI, resolvePromise;
// The Promise and handler
def = new $.Deferred();

updateUI = function (data) {
    $('p').html('I got the data!');
    $('div').html(data);
};
getData = $.ajax({
        url: '/echo/html/',
        data: {
            html: 'testhtml',
            delay: 3
        },
        type: 'post'
    })
    .done(function(resp) {
        return resp;
    })
    .fail(function (error) {
        throw new Error("Error getting the data");
    });


// Event Handler
resolvePromise = function (ev) {
    ev.preventDefault();
    def.resolve(ev.type, this);
```

```
        return def.promise();
};

// Bind the Event
$(document).on('click', 'button', resolvePromise);

def.then(function() {
    return getData;
})
.then(function(data) {
    updateUI(data);
})
.done(function(promiseValue, el) {
    console.log('The promise was resolved by: ', promiseValue, ' on ',
el);
});
// Console output: The promise was resolved by: click on <button>
</button>
```

The reference of the following code is available at `http://jsfiddle.net/`
`cwebbdesign/NEssP/2.`

What promises prescribed not to do

Promises clearly outline what not to do while implementing a promises paradigm.
We saw most of these rules in *Chapter 2, The JavaScript Asynchronous Model*. Let's
take a look at these from the promises paradigm in order to refresh our memories.

The following two practices must be taken into account while implementing
promises, regardless of what implementation you are using:

- Avoiding getting into a callback hell
- Avoiding use of unnamed promises

Avoiding getting into callback hell

We are already aware what callbacks are and how to handle them. Callbacks are
a great way to implement an asynchronous model, but they have their own cost.
They are unmanageable at some point, and that point comes in when you start your
descent in callbacks. The deeper you dive in, the more difficult it becomes to handle,
thus leading you into a callback hell scenario.

All of the promises implementations have sorted this problem very simply and wisely.

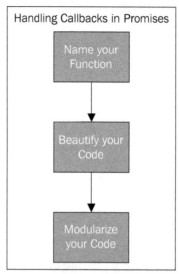

A handy way to tackle callback hell

Avoiding the use of unnamed promises

As we saw from *Chapter 2, The JavaScript Asynchronous Model,* the use of unnamed promises can cause huge problems and will cost more time than the normal function of writing and testing. In some instances, it's good and recommended that you do not give the name of your function, but it's not good practice to leave your promise unnamed.

If someone thinks anonymous functions are hard to deal with, then unreasonably named functions are hard to understand and maintain. I recommend that you come up with a proper, predecided naming convention, and it should be done well before writing the actual code. I prefer to use CamelCase notation in Microsoft style, in which the starting name of the function is in lowercase and the connecting name is in uppercase.

Promises and exceptions

Consider a function that throws exceptions within the promise paradigm. You won't find any trace or log if you try to see what has happened to the exception-throwing function. You will see no output on the screen or on console. Why? The reason is hidden in the basics of promise.

Promises are designed to produce two types of output—a promise will either be fulfilled or rejected. So naturally, it won't show up anywhere at the output streams since promises are not designed to produce any other output except these two predefined states. However, it's not promise that does not give any facility to handle exceptions. In fact, it provides a robust way to show and handle such exceptions, by implementing a proper handler to catch the exception and display the reason at any desirable output stream.

In most of the promises paradigm, the exception is handled by `fail` and `then`. The handlers differ from one library to another and from one language to another language. In many advance high-level languages, error and exception handling are managed automatically without adding much of code and explicitly telling compiler/ interpreter, but in those libraries and languages, in which it's not handled on auto-basis, you have to write an explicit code to handle exception manually.

At this point, it's significant to mention that we are using a bit of code from Q, just to make you understand that exemption handling is also a part of promises implementation and how to deal with an exception, if one occurs. In our next chapter, we will focus more on how to implement promises in other libraries and languages.

Coming back to the topic, like many other implementations, Q has its own mechanism of dealing with promises.

Consider that this code is about to throw an exception:

```
function imException()
{
throw "imException";

}//end of code
```

Since it's not the right implementation of handling exception in promises using Q, there will be no output at all, and if we want to handle it as per implementation of the Promises paradigm in Q, we will want to add a rejection handler.

Let's take Q as an example, in order to see if we can add the same function using its `fcall()` method:

```
Q.fcall(imException);
```

This method call is not meant to handle the exceptions, so it won't show anything. To handle it, we need to add a rejection handler that will help us to track and monitor the exception.

The fail method

The simplest way to handle exception is using `fail`. Let's restructure our code to implement the `fail` method:

```
// code view before exception handler
Q.fcall(imException);

//code after exception handler
Q.fcall(imException) .fail(function(err) { console.log(err); });
```

The then method

Normally, we would use `then` to handle chaining promise. This will take two arguments and the return promise-based execution of one of these handlers:

```
Q.fcall(imException)
.then(
    // first handler-fulfill
    function() { },

    // second handler -reject
    function(err) {
        console.log(err);
    }
);
```

The first argument was a fulfill method and the second is rejection handler, as shown in the preceding code. Using these simple techniques, Q implements exception handling.

Best practices to handle exceptions in promise

Promise provides an impressive way to handle exceptions. Exception handling in promise is quite simple and easy to implement, and almost all libraries and implementations support a generic way of implementation. Here are some of best practices to deal with exceptions:

Make your exceptions meaningful

To maximize performance and maintainability, throw understandable errors. The best practice is to reject a promise and reject it with an error instance. Make it a habit not to reject an error object or primitive values.

Monitor, anticipate, and handle exception

Keep an eye on the effects of errors on the flow of execution. The best practice for doing this is to anticipate failures in your handlers. The better you are at anticipation, the better will be your control over the flow of execution. Always think whether your rejection handler should be invoked by failures in the resolution handler, or if there should be a different behavior.

Keep it clean

When you are done dealing with exception, start CleanUp as soon as the error occurs. When the chain of promises is processed and a result has been delivered in either rejected or fulfilled state, terminate the chain and clean up the unused thread. This will help in not only optimizing the throughput of code, but also creating manageable outputs.

Mozilla has its own implementation for handling errors in promise, which can be seen at `https://developer.mozilla.org/en-US/docs/Mozilla/JavaScript_code_modules/Promise.jsm/Promise`.

Considerations while choosing a promise

Before you start working with a promise library, there are a number of elements you should keep in mind. Not all the implementations of a promise's implementation are created equally. They are different from one another in terms of offered utilities by API, performance, and sometimes, behavior too.

A promise/proposal just outlines the proposed behavior of the promises and not implementation specifications. This results in varying libraries offering a different set of features. These are the ways that they differ from one another:

- All promises/compliments have `then();` function and also have varying features in their API. In addition to this, they're still able to exchange promises with each other.

- In promise/compliant libraries, a thrown exception is translated into a rejection and the `errorHandler()` method is called with the exception.

As a result of the differing implementations, there are interoperability problems when working with libraries that return or expect promise/compliant.

There may be trade-offs in choosing a promise library. Every library has its own pros and cons, and it is purely up to you to decide what to use depending on the particular use case and your project needs.

Summary

In this chapter, we covered the paradigm of promise and the concept behind it. We have covered the conceptual knowledge of promise, deferred, common sequences of promise, and how promise helps in decoupling the business logic and application logic. We have also covered the relation between promise and event emitters and the idea behind it.

Due to the virtue of this chapter, we are now able the select which promise library we should use on the basis of our knowledge gained.

In our next chapter, we will be looking at the implementation of promise in different programming languages and will examine the ease they are bringing for the developers and end users.

4
Implementing Promises

In the last chapter, *Chapter 3, The Promise Paradigm,* we have seen how promise and its theories were fabricated together to form a whole new amazing picture of the software engineering paradigm, and especially in today's modern asynchronous application development life cycle.

In this chapter, we will start experimenting on how this concept can take shape by implementing promises in real time. Why do we need to see its implementation? The answer to this question is quite simple; we need to see how the concept we have developed so far is true and how much of this concept is really applicable. Also, with these little implementations of promises, we will plot the base of our foundation to use promise in other technologies in later chapters. So, let's see how we will go about with this implementation phase.

How to implement promises

So far, we have learned the concept of promise, its basic ingredients, and some of the basic functions it has to offer in nearly all of its implementations, but how are these implementations using it? Well, it's quite simple. Every implementation, either in the language or in the form of a library, maps the basic concept of promises. It then maps it to a compiler/interpreter or in code. This allows the written code or functions to behave in the paradigm of promise, which ultimately presents its implementations.

Promises are now part of the standard package for many languages. The obvious thing is that they have implemented it in their own way as per the need. We will be examining more on how these languages are implementing the concept of promise in detail in this chapter.

Implementations in Java

Java is among the world's favorite and most admired programming languages and is used in millions of devices across the globe. There is no need to say anything further about Java, except that it's the first choice of engineers when it comes to creating application software that uses multithreaded and controlled asynchronous patterns and behaviors. Java is one of the few languages that has implemented asynchronous behavior by default in its compiler, which helps programmers to write robust, scalable, and maintainable pieces of software.

The util package of Java

Naturally, Java has more acceptability for the concept of promise and its implementation. There are many implementations in the package of java.util. concurrent, regarding promise and its implementations. We have handpicked some of the interfaces and classes that are helping out in implementing promises or nearly matching the concept.

The mechanics of Java to implement a promise

Within the java.util.concurrent package, there are a number of interfaces and classes that will help us to write concurrent and asynchronous code, but there are a few particular interfaces and libraries that are specific to this promise/ future implementation.

The java.util.concurrent package is home to concurrent programming (as the name says) and is the home of few small standardized extensible frameworks. This also helps in implementing some of the core classes, which in normal conditions, are hard to work with.

The core components of java.util.concurrent

The `java.util.concurrent` package has many classes and components, but some of the core components that make this particular package more adaptable to work are:

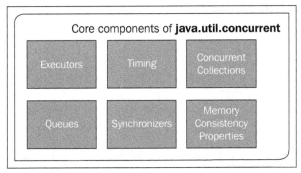

Core components of the Java util.concurrent package

Executor

`Executor` is a simple standardized interface, which is commonly used to define custom threaded subsystems. These subsystems include the thread pools, asynchronous I/O, and task-based lighter frameworks.

Tasks created in the thread can either be executed in "the same task-execution thread" or in a new thread; this may also be executed in the thread calling execute sequentially or concurrently. Whichever thread the execute pattern task adopts is purely based on the concrete `Executor` class used.

The `ExecutiveService` interface provides a fully stacked asynchronous tasks framework. This interface is for a number of tasks of the pool, which includes the controlled shutdown of `Executor`, managing of different in-pool cues, and scheduling of tasks. There are a few more associates that work with `ExecutiveService` to add support to delay the periodic and periodic task executing. One such associate is `ScheduledExecutorService`, a subinterface that works with the `ExecutiveService` interface in managing the delayed and periodic tasks executing whenever called upon.

There is another interface called the `ExecutorService` interface, which provides methods to arrange the execution of any function that is expressed as callable.

Queues

When it comes to the queue, the only thought that first emerges is the pattern of **First In First Out** (FIFO). Just as other languages apply this data structure in their own ways, Java treats it as an efficient and scalable thread-safe, nonblocking FIFO queue by employing the `ConcurrentLinkedQueue` class from its `java.util.concurrent` package. In the same package, five implementations support the `BlockingQueue` interface.

The `BlockingQueue` interface is a queue, which has an advanced wait mechanism. This holds the queue to further get into processing until all the previous processing is done. This also waits for the space to make the queue available when storing an element.

The five implementations of the `BlockingQueue` interface are listed as follows:

- `LinkedBlockingQueue`
- `ArrayBlockingQueue`
- `SynchronousQueue`
- `PriorityBlockingQueue`
- `DelayQueue`

We will discuss some of these relevant implementations in the following section.

Timing

Since `util` is the utilities package, it has controls in the form of classes and interfaces that help engineers to make use of their daily routine stuff. One such package is the timing of a method or interface. This is to perform certain instructed operations, and eventually, they time out themselves once the operation is done.

Most of us are already aware of the importance of session creation and session timeout, especially those of us who are programmers for the Web. Session tracking is a subject in its own and doesn't really link that much from the structure of this chapter, so we will return our focus to the topic of timing.

This packing is like a timing belt of Java programs. In any engine, the role of a timing belt is to make sure that certain mechanical operations are done within a specified amount of time; it is the same as with this package. This controls the in-time and out-time of functions and also the definite/indefinite waits. The point to remember is that all these methods use the time out in every case. This helps threads define the amount of time a method spends within a thread pool and saves the actual program to perform with scalability.

Synchronizers

Java provides a low-level thread creation and execution so that programmers can easily handle and modify the thread-level control. In earlier versions, the controlling of threads was considered the hardest topic to deal with, as there was much of the manual control than automation of threads and their synchronization. At this time, Java was much more advanced in controlling multiple threads than its competing languages, but still playing with threads was a fairly hard task for Java engineers.

In the later versions of Java, this problem was considered as the most important one to find a regulation, and finally, with the emergence of version 7, the compiler has fixed most of the problems faced by engineers.

In the current version, which is version 8, five classes aid the purpose of synchronization:

- The `Semaphore` class is a classic concurrency tool and has been around for a very long time (http://docs.oracle.com/javase/7/docs/api/java/util/concurrent/Semaphore.html)
- The `CountDownLatch` class is a very simple yet common utility for blocking until a given number of signals, events, or operations being performed in other thread are being taken care off (http://docs.oracle.com/javase/7/docs/api/java/util/concurrent/CountDownLatch.html)
- The `CyclicBarrier` class is a resettable multiway synchronization point, which is useful in some styles of parallel programming (http://docs.oracle.com/javase/7/docs/api/java/util/concurrent/CyclicBarrier.html)
- The `Phaser` class provides a more flexible form of barrier that may be used to control phased computation among multiple threads (http://docs.oracle.com/javase/7/docs/api/java/util/concurrent/Phaser.html)
- The `Exchanger` class allows two threads to exchange objects at a rendezvous point and is useful in several pipeline designs (http://docs.oracle.com/javase/7/docs/api/java/util/concurrent/Exchanger.html)

Concurrent collections

The `Concurrent` packages provide the implementations for a multithreaded context and has the following implementations.

Since it has more specific sync facilities, some of its classes use the prefix `Concurrent` to highlight the additional facilitates it is providing. A few more prominent ones are:

- `ConcurrentHashMap`
- `ConcurrentSkipListMap`

- ConcurrentSkipListSet
- CopyOnWriteArrayList
- CopyOnWriteArraySet

The virtue of concurrent collection is its safe thread, but not overlooked by a single locking mechanism, in particular. Only in the case of ConcurrentHashMap, it allows any sum of concurrent reads as well as concurrent writes. Why, then, do we use synchronized classes? The answer is that they are very useful in preventing all the access to a collection using a single lock, but it has a cost, and poorer scalability.

In other cases where multiple threads are in line to access a common collection, the current version of classes is more advisable, whereas unsynchronized locks are used when either collections are unshared or they can be accessed when holding other locks.

The implementation of promise by Java

Java implements the paradigm of promise using its promising class and interfaces. Although its asynchronous behavior is one of the core and flagship features of Java, here are the ingredients of how promise is implemented in Java:

- Interfaces:
    - CompletionService
    - ExecutorService
    - Future
- Classes:
    - Delayed
    - DelayQueue
    - FutureTask

CompletionService

The CompletionService interface acts as a service to make a distinction between new asynchronous tasks from the result of completed tasks. This follows a simple process in which the producer adds the tasks for execution. For the consumers, this interface takes completed tasks and processes their results in the order that they were marked as completed. This service can be used for many concurrent operations, such as managing an asynchronous I/O. The mechanism of an asynchronous I/O is the tasks that are submitted in one part of the program or set of programs or in a system, and then acted upon the different parts of the program. The submission order may be different than the order they were requested initially.

The mechanism of an asynchronous I/O is that it reads tasks and stores it in one part of the program, such as buffer.

This can be a single program (such as browser) or a set of programs (such as an operating system thread pool). The thread handler decides which thread needs to be executed first.

This interface relies on a separate executor or actually executes the tasks due to which the `CompletionService` interface only manages an internal completion queue. As interfaces implement, they need a class to do so, and the `ExecutorCompletionService` class provides such a facility.

ExecutorService

The `ExecutorService` interface has two main roles to perform—one is to provide methods to manage the termination of asynchronous tasks, and the other is to provide the methods that can produce a future value for tracing. This tracking can be done for either one or more asynchronous tasks.

The use of an `Executor` for `ExecutorService`:

- `ExecutorService` inherits `Executor`, which provides the methods to manage termination and production of a future value to track the progress.
- `ExecutorService` when shutdown rejects all the new tasks. They have been loaded with two different methods:
    - `shutdown()`
    - `shutdownNow()`

The `shutdown()` method allows the tasks in memory to conclude their states and then terminate them. Also, it prevents the memory from entering and processing it for any upcoming tasks. On the other hand, `shutdownnow()` doesn't give any such liberty; it just terminates whatever is in the memory, then and there. This also totally rejects the entry of new tasks in the memory by nullifying the existing thread.

Both the methods have their own significance, but since both are related to termination of existing tasks, they must be used with much care and with proper understanding of the potential consequences.

The following code snippet is taken from the original Java docs, which is available at http://docs.oracle.com/javase/7/docs/api/java/util/concurrent/ExecutorService.html:

```
class NetworkService implements Runnable {
  private final ServerSocket serverSocket;
```

```
    private final ExecutorService pool;

    public NetworkService(int port, int poolSize)
    throws IOException {
      serverSocket = new ServerSocket(port);
      pool = Executors.newFixedThreadPool(poolSize);
    }

    public void run() { // run the service
      try {
        for (;;) {
          pool.execute(new Handler(serverSocket.accept()));
        }
      } catch (IOException ex) {
        pool.shutdown();
      }
    }
  }

  class Handler implements Runnable {
    private final Socket socket;
    Handler(Socket socket) { this.socket = socket; }
    public void run() {
      // read and service request on socket
    }
  }
```

The following method shuts down an `ExecutorService` interface in two phases: first, by calling shutdown to reject incoming tasks, and then by calling shutdownNow(), if necessary, to cancel any lingering tasks:

```
void shutdownAndAwaitTermination(ExecutorService pool) {
  pool.shutdown(); // Disable new tasks from being submitted
  try {
    // Wait a while for existing tasks to terminate
    if (!pool.awaitTermination(60, TimeUnit.SECONDS)) {
      pool.shutdownNow(); // Cancel currently executing tasks
      // Wait a while for tasks to respond to being cancelled
      if (!pool.awaitTermination(60, TimeUnit.SECONDS))
        System.err.println("Pool did not terminate");
    }
  } catch (InterruptedException ie) {
    // (Re-)Cancel if current thread also interrupted
```

```
    pool.shutdownNow();
    // Preserve interrupt status
    Thread.currentThread().interrupt();
  }
}
```

Future

In Java, `future` represents the value of the result of an asynchronous computation. Methods are provided to track the status of result. These methods indicate whether the current state is waiting or not.

The catch is, you can only yield the result using `get` or when the computation is done.

Cancellation can be done via the cancel method; this sounds very easy to remember. Cancellation of a `Future` value can be done using the cancellation method.

You can also check whether the task was completed normally or cancelled by virtue of this method invocation. Once the computation is done, it cannot be cancelled; this sounds so promising to us, just like the concept of promise.

You can also use `Future` to cancel tasks. Although it's not a very good approach, if you want to do it, then you can declare many types of `Future` objects and ask the method to return null; that's it! You got your task cancelled once again. This must be done before the final computation of the tasks.

Here is the code snippet:

```
interface ArchiveSearcher { String search(String target); }

class App {

  ExecutorService executor = ...ArchiveSearcher searcher = ...
  void showSearch(final String target)
  throws InterruptedException {
    Future<String> future
    = executor.submit(new Callable<String>() {
      public String call() {
        return searcher.search(target);
      }});
    displayOtherThings(); // do other things while searching
    try {
```

```
        displayText(future.get()); // use future
    } catch (ExecutionException ex) { cleanup(); return; }
    }
}
```

The `FutureTask` class is an implementation of `Future` that implements `Runnable`, and so may be executed by an `Executor`. For example, the previous construction with submit can be replaced by the following:

```
FutureTask<String> future =
    new FutureTask<String>(new Callable<String>() {
        public String call() {
        return searcher.search(target);
    }});
executor.execute(future);
```

Delay and DelayedQueue

`Delay` is an interface that uses a marker to mark those objects that were acted upon, after they were given a delay.

`DelayedQueue` is an unbounded queue that is used to collect all the objects that were delayed/expired. Since it's a queue, it must have a header element whose delay has expired long ago.

Since it's a queue and is similar to a `queue` data structure, it has a starting point called header and an ending point called footer. When it comes to future, the queue we are referring to here has a value, which has already expired due to the failed promise or unfulfilled promise.

If such an element was not found, will the poll return null when the expiration occurs? Well, it occurs when the method `getDelay(TimeUnit.NANOSECONDS)` returns the value as less than or equal to zero. The expired elements in this way cannot be removed, so they are treated as normal ones.

FutureTask

`FutureTask` is the cancellable asynchronous computation. This is the basic provider of `Future` that is loaded with methods from start of a method to cancel it. This also helps in the retrieving of the result of the computation, and since it's an implementation, the result can be extracted when the computation has been completed. Needless to mention that once the result is computed, it cannot be pulled back or changed as it's a promise.

Summing up Java and Promises.js

If we conclude the preceding discussion, it's clear that Java has a clearer approach and implementation when it comes to Promises.js. It's a mature way of handling asynchronous behavior, and especially, the way it handles multithreading is far better than what other languages have to offer. However, as every implementation has its own drawbacks, Java too has it, and it's quite acceptable since you cannot just copy and paste the theory as it is with any compiler/interpreter. There are few more supportive frameworks/libraries contributed by an open source community to add the remainder of its implementation.

Say hello to JDeferred

Inspired by the implementation of promise in jQuery, few Java Engineers have started to develop a library called `JDeferred`. This implements the concept of promise as robustly as it should be by leaving the gaping holes of the `java.util. concurrent` package. This was a brief of how `JDeferred` works. Let's dive deep into what it is and its unique advantages, as compared to other implantations available in the market.

Just like jQuery has a deferred object, `JDeferred` is designed in a similar way to behave and contact with Java's compiler. `JDeferred` is not only similar with jQuery's implementation of promise, but it also extends its support to the Android Deferred Object. *Chapter 8, Promises in jQuery* is the dedicated chapter on jQuery and its mechanism and working on promise, so we can skip that part for now and see what the Android Deferred Object is, and how it fits into the implementation of promise.

A few words about Android Deferred Object

It would be unfair not to showcase the existence of Android Deferred Object and its properties when we are discussing `JDeferred`. The Android Deferred Object is a utility or more simply, it is a chainable utility object that can actually do all the same stuff for the Android domain. It can register multiple callbacks in a single callback queue; it can invoke callback queues and after processing. It also can relay the state of success or failure to whichever function is waiting for; it doesn't matter whether it's a synchronous function or an asynchronous function.

Its working is quite straightforward. You obtain a promise out of a function that was executed asynchronously. As we can work around with promise, you can attach callbacks to get notified about the success or failure. Whenever this piece of program that was working asynchronously finishes off as expected, the promise is called to be resolved in case of any error; it calls the `rejected` parameter.

Use case 1 – object success and failure callbacks for a task

Say that you need an asynchronous HTTP request. A simple way of using Android Deferred Object is to wrap the request in to `DeferredAsyncTask` and attach callbacks to your action. Here is the code for such a scenario:

```
new DeferredAsyncTask<HttpResponse,HttpResponse,Void>() {
  protected abstract Resolved doInBackground() throws Exception {
    //do your async code here
  }
}
.done( new ResolveCallback<HttpResponse> {
  public void onResolve(HttpResponse resolved) {
    //your success code here
  }
})
.fail ( new RejectCallback<HttpResponse> {
  public void onReject(HttpResponse rejected) {
      //your failure code here
  }
});
```

The reference to preceding code is available at `https://github.com/CodeAndMagic/android-deferred-object`.

Use case 2 – merging several promises

This use case is best for when you need to add several executed promises into a single one by merging them as a single promise. A convenient way is to call the `DeferredObject.when` method:

```
Promise<A1,B1,C1> p1 = new DeferredAsyncTask<A1,B1,C1>() { ... };
Promise<A2,B2,C2> p1 = new DeferredAsyncTask<A2,B2,C2>() { ... };
Promise<A3,B3,C3> p3 = new DeferredAsyncTask<A3,B3,C3>() { ... };
//when gives you a new promise that gets triggered when all the merged
promises are resolved or one of them fails
DeferredObject.when(p1,p2,p3)
.done(new ResolveCallback<MergedPromiseResult3<A1,A2,A3>() {
  public void onResolve(MergedPromiseResult3<A1,A2,A3> resolved){
    Log.i(TAG, "got: " + resolved.first() + resolved.second() +
    resolved.third());
  }
})
```

```
.fail(new RejectCallback<MergedPromiseReject>() {
  public void onReject(MergedPromiseReject rejected) {
    //failure handling here
  }
})
.progress(new ProgressCallback<MergedPromiseProgress>() {
  public void onProgress(final MergedPromiseProgress progress){
    //you get notified as the merged promises keep coming in
  }
});
//Merging doesn't stop you do add individual callbacks for promises
that are in the merge
p1.done(...).fail(...)
//Or even merging them in another way
DeferredObject.when(p1,p2).done(...).fail(...)
```

Mechanics of JDeferred

Coming back to our core discussion of JDeferred, there is almost everything that this implementation has adopted from promises and considered to be more promised than any other library. We will look at what the features it's providing are, and how they are implemented within.

Features of JDeferred

The implementation of JDeferred provides all the methods needed to present the promise paradigm in Java. This has features such as deferred objects and promise, promise callbacks, multiple promises, callable and runnable methods, and Java's generic support.

The following table summarizes the features, along with their available implementation:

Feature	Available implementation
Deferred object and promise	N/A
Promise callbacks	.then(...)
	.done(...)
	.fail(...)
	.progress(...)
	.always(...)

Feature	Available implementation
Multiple promises	`.when(p1, p2, p3, ...).then(...)`
Callable and runnable wrappers	`.when(new Runnable() {...})`
Java generic support	`Deferred<Integer, Exception, Double> deferred;` `deferred.resolve(10);` `deferred.reject(new Exception());` `deferred.progress(0.80);`

Playing with the code using JDeferred

We will now explore some of the common examples of this implementation, which are used most often. We will be looking at the following topics:

- Deferred object and promise
- Deferred Manager
- Runnable and callable
- `wait()` and `waitSafely()`
- Filters
- Pipes

Deferred object and promise

The following code will help you understand how `JDeferred` implements deferred objects and promise. This code has comments for a better understanding:

```
//creating new deferred object by calling method DeferredObject();

Deferred deferredObj = new DeferredObject();

//now its time to make some promise
Promise promise = deferredObj.promise();

promise.done(new DoneCallback() {

    public void onDone(Object result) {
```

```
    //some code here
  }

}).fail(new FailCallback() {
  public void onFail(Object rejection) {
    //some more code
  }
}).progress(new ProgressCallback() {
  public void onProgress(Object progress) {
    //some code here


  }
}).always(new AlwaysCallback() {
  public void onAlways(State state, Object result, Object
  rejection) {
    //some code here


  }
});
```

Deferred Manager

Deferred Manager is a simple way to manage your deferred objects. Call the default
method of Deferred Manager, and then add the number of promises you want:

```
//create Deferred Manager's object
DeferredManager theDeferredManager = new DefaultDeferredManager();

// uncomment this to specify Executor

// DeferredManager theDeferredManager = new
DefaultDeferredManager(myExecutorService);


//add and initialize number of promises

Promise pm1, pm2, pm3;
theDeferredManager.when(p1, p2, p3)

// or you can add here .done(…)
//or you can add the fail here using    .fail(…)
```

Runnable and callable

Runnable and callable, which is as good as promise, can be used as follows:

```
DeferredManager theDeferredManager = new DefaultDeferredManager();

theDeferredManager.when(new Callable<Integer>()

{
  public Integer call() {
    // return something
    // or throw a new exception
  }
}).done(new DoneCallback<Integer>() {
  public void onDone(Integer result) {
    ...
  }
}).fail(new FailCallback<Throwable>() {
  public void onFail(Throwable e) {
    ...
  }
});
```

You can use `DeferredCallable` and `DeferredRunnable` if you want to do the following:

- Be notified about the progress made by the callable or runnable
- You want to make your `Deferred` object

Here is an example code:

```
final Deferred deferred = ...
Promise ThePromise = deferred.promise();
ThePromise.then(…);

Runnable runable = new Runnable() {

  public void run() {
    while (…) {
      deferred.notify(myProgress);
    }
```

```
      deferred.resolve("done");
    }
  }
}
```

Extending `DeferredRunnable`:

```
DeferredManager theDeferredManager = …;
theDeferredManager.when(new DeferredRunnable<Double>(){
  public void run() {
    while (…) {
      notify(myProgress);
    }
  }
}).then(…);
```

wait() and waitSafely()

The `wait()` and `waitSafely()` functions are the part of `JDeferred` that wants to assume the control of all asynchronous tasks. This is not recommended, but can be very useful in some cases:

```
Promise promise = theDeferredManager.when(...)
  .done(...) //when done
  .fail(...) // when fail

synchronized (p)
  while (promise.isPending()) {
    try {
      promise.wait();
    } catch (InterruptedException e) { ... }
  }
}
```

The shortcut to the preceding code is as follows:

```
Promise promise = theDeferredManager.when(...)
  .done(...)
  .fail(...)

try {
  promise.waitSafely(); //replaced waitSafely();
} catch (InterruptedException e) {
  ...
}
```

Filters

Here is the code that we will use for the filtration of promise and deferred objects:

```
Deferred d = …;
Promise promise = d.promise();
Promise filtered = promise.then(new DoneFilter<Integer, Integer>() {
  public Integer filterDone(Integer result)
    return result * 10;
  }
});

filtered.done(new DoneCallback<Integer>{
  public void onDone(Integer result) {
    // result would be original * 10
```

Pipes

Pipes in JDeferred also act for the asynchronous computation of tasks within the ordered manner:

```
Deferred d = ...;
Promise promise = d.promise();

promise.then(new DonePipe<Integer, Integer, Exception, Void>() {
  public Deferred<Integer, Exception, Void> pipeDone(Integer
  result) {
    if (result < 100) {
      return new DeferredObject<Integer, Void,
      Void>().resolve(result);
    } else {
      return new DeferredObject<Integer, Void, Void>().reject(new
      Exception(...));
    }
  }
}).done(...).fail(...);

d.resolve(80) -> done!
d.resolve(100) -> fail!
```

Ultimate JDeferred

As you have seen, it's a much more powerful implementation of Java using promise. Java is very powerful when it comes to implementing the promise paradigm.

Actually, Java itself has many powerful features, but when it comes to proper implementation, such frameworks help us out. Since they are community maintained, they have a problem in terms of quality, as you may find nontested and unverified code that can waste your time. However, JDeferred has almost identical implementation, compared to jQuery.

Summary

Within this chapter of the book, we have actually started our journey towards mastering the promise. This chapter covered why we are implementing promise and why we chose Java as the core of this chapter. Java has richer features than any other programming language and it's also tried very well to keep it more or less similar to the automation of asynchronous behavior. We explored the core components of Java's util.concurrent class in greater detail and by virtue of which we have seen many live examples from Java docs online. Since Java cannot implement the promise paradigm in whole due to the limitations that we have seen, an open source library that acts exactly the same as the promise's paradigm has prescribed it. JDeferred has cleared the rest of the doubts out of our minds by taking full advantage of implementing the core values of promise, such as future, deferred, and so on.

In the next chapter, we will carry out a more practical work to develop our understanding of promise with WinRT.

5

Promises in WinRT

In last four chapters, we spent time making our concept strong and our foundation of thoughts aligned to promise. From this chapter onwards, we will explore promise in different technologies. We will see how these technologies adopted the concept, the reasons why thy adopted it, and how long promise has been associated with these technologies. We will sample some of the code bases of related technologies in order to get firsthand knowledge on how to actually implement promise in real time.

An introduction to WinRT

Our first lookout for the technology is WinRT. What is WinRT? It is the short form for Windows Runtime. This is a platform provided by Microsoft to build applications for Windows 8+ operating system. It supports application development in C++/ICX, C# (C sharp), VB.NET, TypeScript, and JavaScript.

Microsoft adopted JavaScript as one of its prime and first-class tools to develop cross-browser apps and for the development on other related devices. We are now fully aware of what the pros and cons of using JavaScript are, which has brought us here to implement the use of promise.

You guessed it right! In this chapter, we will focus on how promise is implemented on WinRT, which was the need of implementation, and how it's implemented. We will also sample some code wherever needed to see how well promise is helping in this platform, and how one can actually use it.

The evolution of WinRT

With the announcement of Windows 8, Microsoft has released a complete new architecture of its famous and most used operating system, Windows. This architecture is for all the devices and platforms, including mobile phones, tablets, wearable, and so on. Due to this singleton approach, a unified approach for application development was very much needed, so Microsoft included a few more tools and languages in its platform, and from there JavaScript for Windows, or Win, came on to the scene.

You may ask why have they adopted JavaScript and why not some other language for their expanding arsenal of web programming? The answer lies in the architecture of JavaScript. In the previous chapters, we learned how JavaScript is considered to be the best tool for web-based programming and how it's useful in many scenarios. Microsoft has adopted this power and embedded it into its WinRT platform. By adding this, Microsoft has an edge over many of its competitors, as it now has access to a wider range of programmers who know that JavaScript can also program for Microsoft and show their work to a large number of users.

A little detail about WinJS

WinJS was released as an open source JavaScript library, which was released by Microsoft under the Apache License. It was initially aimed to be used for building the software for Windows app store, but later, it became widely accepted to port on all browsers. Now, it is used in combination with HTML5 to build apps for both brewers-based and for windows app store.

It was first announced on April 4, 2014, at the Microsoft Build conference 2014, and since then it has seen an evolution from version 1.0 to 3.0 with loads of functions and implementations within its SDK.

WinJS – its purpose and a distribution history

WinJS 1.0 was first released with Windows 8.0. Here are its notable distributions up until now. The distribution history is as follows:

The distribution name	Purpose/focused area
WinJS 1.0	This was released as the JavaScript library for Windows 8.0.
WinJS 2.0 for Windows 8.1	This is an updated version and released under Apache License at GitHub.
WinJS Xbox 1.0 for Windows	This was an exclusive release for Xbox one for Windows.
WinJS Phone 2.1 for Windows Phone 8.1	This was released for Windows phone development platform.
WinJS 3.0	This was released in September 2014 for improved cross-platform functionality, JavaScript modularization, and improvements in a universal control design.

WinJS on GitHub

Since WinJS is an open source software, it's hosted on GitHub as MSTF, Microsoft Open Technologies. I presume that you are aware of what GitHub is and what it's used for; if not, check out `https://github.com/`.

The online repository of WinJS has three basic divisions:

- WinJS, which is written in TypeScript and can be found at `https://github.com/winjs/winjs`

- WinJS modules that are written in JS and can be seen at `https://github.com/winjs/winjs-modules`

- The WinJS browser, which is also written in JS and be found at `https://github.com/winjs/winjs-browser`

Code in these repository is constantly updated and bug fixes are committed by programmers around the globe 24 x 7, which is the sole beauty of open source projects. The base repository is located at `https://github.com/winjs`.

With online emulators, you can try WinJS at `http://try.buildwinjs.com`.

HTML5, CSS3, and JavaScript

HTML5, CSS3, and JS are a de facto model for web app development, for one strong reason. They all are more than technologies: they are standards. There were times when companies were in the habit of introducing their own platform, and with many bounties, they offered to programmers to use their platforms. Back in those days, keeping a standard for the application on all browsers was a nightmare for developers, and hence a lot of time was consumed on projects for their compatibility rather than their actual feature development. This frustration was addressed by W3C and other standard maintaining bodies and started to work on standardsthat would be acceptable for all the major game players of the industry. They will use these as their base, rather than developing their own standard for every tiny need. This caused the evolution of HTML5 and CSS3. Since JavaScript was around already and was considered to be the language of the browser, it was combined with the remaining two to become a default technology bundle for both proprietary and open source projects.

Now, with every platform, these can be used but with a very little difference in syntax. This came as a relief to the programmers and engineers as they could now focus on solving business problems rather than compatibility.

WT with HTML5, CSS3, and JavaScript

JavaScript in WT allows programmers to build apps using HTML and CSS. A lot of WT apps using JavaScript are as same as writing markups for the website. In addition to this, JavaScript on WT provides some additional features and introduces some different ways that you can use it under this platform. Since the implementation of JavaScript varies from platform to platform in WT, it's more or less in the Microsoft style where, with default JS properties available, WT adds some extra features for JavaScript. This provides the enhanced support of touch, more control over the look and feel of the UI (user interface). This also provides controls such as `DatePicker`, `TimePicker`, and `ListView`, and an exclusive access to WinJS.

The need for integrating promise with WT

JS is one of the primary languages on the WT platform. Besides the benefits of JS, there are some drawbacks too. We all know from our discussion in the previous chapter that callback hell was the core reason why there was a need to add promise into it, and the same goes here. WT also faced the same problem, but was quick enough to solve it by implementing promise into it. Promise in JS for WT is the game changer when it comes to writing robust, scalable, and maintainable apps for the Windows platform. Although WT was not the first one that implemented promise, but it is one of the quicker adopters of the concept and implementer.

In fact, JavaScript programmers started using WT JS for Windows, and due to the fact that it's highly adoptable, many more professionals are joining that community.

Problems when using asynchronous programming

Just to refresh your memory, in *Chapter 2, The JavaScript Asynchronous Model*, we learned a great deal on asynchronous programming, what it is, and how JS implements it. We all know that the problem in using JS is the level of complexity it has developed, as it's heavily dependent on the callbacks for most of its operations. In the *Handling callback hell* section of *Chapter 2, The JavaScript Asynchronous Model*, we saw that it's nearly impossible to debug the code if callbacks were getting out of control. The promise paradigm was then called in to solve this problem. The same occurrences are with JS when applied at WT.

Jumpstarting promises

Asynchronous APIs in the Windows library for JS are represented as promises, as defined by common JS promises/proposals. One can make his/her code more robust by including an error handler, and this is considered to be the most important aspect of debugging, and because of this many more JavaScript developers are preferring to use promises.

There is a prerequisite for this jumpstart.

Writing a function that returns a promise

The following is a sample code using which you can develop a good understanding on how to implement the promises in WT effectively. Follow these steps:

1. Create a blank Windows Runtime app named `IamPromise`.
2. Add an `input` element.
3. Add a `div` element that displays the result for the URL.
4. Add styling instructions to `default.css` to add some presentation in the app.
5. Add a change handler for the `input` element.
6. In the change handler, call `xhr`.
7. Build and debug the app, and then enter a URL.

8. Create a WT app in JS in VS2013.

9. Add an `input` element.

10. Within HTML, create an `input` element using the following code:

```
<div>
<input id="inputUrl" />
<!—the input id above is called input URL -- >
</div>

Add a DIV element that displays the result for the URL.

<div id="ResultDiv">Result</div>
<!—the div id named here as ResultDiv -- >

Add the styling instructions to "default.css".

input {
   // add your style statements here
}
```

Adding a change handler for input elements

Use the following code to understand the `WinJS.Utilitties.Ready` function, which is called immediately after the event of DOM content being loaded. This is initiated after the page has been parsed, but before all the resources are loaded:

```
WinJS.Utilities.ready(function () {

   // get the element by id
   var input = document.getElementById("inputUrl");
   // add our event listener here
   input.addEventListener("change", changeHandler);

}, false);
```

In the change handler, call `xhr`.

Call `xhr` in the change handler by passing it in the URL that the user entered. Afterwards, update the `div` element with the result. The `xhr` function is the function that returns a promise. We can also use the `then` or `done` function of the promise to update the UI (user interface), but there is a difference between the usage of `then()` and `done()` within WT specification. The `then()` function is executed as soon as the `xhr` function has either returned as a success or an error has been made by `XmlHttpRequest`. On the contrary, the `done()` function is the same except that it is guaranteed to throw any error that is not handled inside the function:

```
function changeHandler(e) {
  var input = e.target;
  var resDiv = document.getElementById("ResultDiv");

  WinJS.xhr({ url: e.target.value }).then(function
  completed(result) {
    if (result.status === 200) {
      resDiv.style.backgroundColor = "lightGreen";
      resDiv.innerText = "Success";
    }
  });
}
```

And finally, it is time to test your code. Build and debug the app and then enter a URL. If the URL is valid, the resultant `div` element, in our case `ResultDiv`, should turn green and display the **Success** message. The code won't do anything if a wrong URL is entered.

 One thing to keep in mind here is that after you enter the URL, a click may be needed outside the input control for the change event to happen. This mostly is not the case, but just for a tip, it is a simpler way to get the future value of promise.

Now, the second best part comes in — handling errors.

Error handling

The best part of using promise is that the error handling and debugging becomes simpler. By simply adding a few functions, you can not only pin point the location of an error in your code, but also get the relevant error log either on the console or on the browser. You don't have to add `alert()` all the time to investigate the nature and location of the error.

The same goes for our previous code, in which we can add an error function inside `then()`. Remember in the previous code where when an error occurred, no error was shown? However, not this time. We will add an error handler, which will change the background color of success to red if any error was found:

```
function changeHandler(e) {
  var input = e.target;
  var resDiv = document.getElementById("ResultDiv");

  WinJS.xhr({url: e.target.value}).then(
    function fulfilled (result) {
      if (result.status === 200) {
        resDiv.style.backgroundColor = "lightGreen";
        resDiv.innerText = "Successfully returned the Promise ";
      }
    },
    // our error handler Function

    function error(e) {
      resDiv.style.backgroundColor = "red";

      if (e.message != undefined) {  // when the URL is incorrect
      or blank.
        resDiv.innerText = e.message;
      }

      else if (e.statusText != undefined) { // If  XmlHttpRequest
      was made.
        resDiv.innerText = e.statusText;
      }

      else {
        resDiv.innerText = "Error";
      }
    });
}
```

Build and debug the app and enter the URL. If the URL was correct, success will be displayed, otherwise the button will turn red and display an error message.

Note that in the preceding function, `error(e)`, we concatenated the e parameter with a message. Use this practice to convert the error into a string, as it will show more understandable messages that will help you to debug and remove errors.

Chaining promises using the then() and done() functions

As with the specifications, you can not only use `then` and `done` functions to achieve a single task, but also for making a chain out of it. In such a way, you can also create your own conditions within the code that will make your code more powerful, optimized, and logical. There are certain limitations though and these are also logical. You can add multiple `then()` such as `then().then().then()`, but you cannot do something like `then().done().then()`. You may be wondering about the logic behind this. With every `then()`, it returns a promise, which you can input to the next `then()` function, but when you add `done()`, it returns `undefined`, which breaks the logic of a promise, yet you will get nothing out of such a chain.

So, in a nutshell, you can do this: `then().then().done()`.

However, you cannot do this: `then().done().then()`.

A generic example of doing such operations can look like this:

```
FirstAsync()
    .then(function () { return SecondAsync(); })
    .then(function () { return ThirdAsync(); })
    .done(function () { finish(); });
```

Also, keep in mind that if you didn't add an error handler to `done()` and the operation has an error, it will throw an exception, which will cost the entire event loop. You won't be able to catch such an exception in a `try catch` block, even if it's written inside the block, and the only way to get it is via `window.onerror()`.

However, this won't be the case when you don't add an error handler with `then()`. It won't throw an exception as it's not designed in this way, instead it will only return a promise in an error state, which can do more harm for the next inline chain or processed output. So add error handlers, whether it's `then()` or `done()`.

Example 1A – downloading a web page to a file using two asynchronous functions

Using this example, we will be able to download a web page to a file. There are several ways to do this. The simplest one is to ask the browser to save the file for you, but that will be the browser's ability to act upon our instructions and not our code's ability to do so. Also, you can imagine how this simple operation can easily explain how to do it by using two asynchronous methods.

Now, have a look at the following code:

```
//WinJs code

WinJS.Utilities.startLog();

// Allocate the URI where to get the download the file.
var AllocatedUri = new Windows.Foundation.UriExample("http://www.
packt.com");

// Get the folder for temporary files.
var temporaryFolder =
Windows.Storage.ApplicationData.current.temporaryFolder;

// Create the temp file asynchronously.
temporaryFolder.createFileAsync("temporary.text",
Windows.Storage.CreationCollisionOption.replaceExisting)
   .then(function (tempFile) {

      // lets start the download operation if the createFileAsync
      call succeeded

      var Iamdownloader = new
      Windows.Networking.BackgroundTransfer.BackgroundDownloader();
      var transfer = Iamdownloader.createDownload(uriExample,
      tempFile);
        return transfer.startAsync();
   })
   .then(

      //Define the function to use when the download completes
      successfully
      function (result) {
        WinJS.log && WinJS.log("File was download successfully ");
      });
```

Again, we will now explain which line is doing what.

There are three main methods to emphasize on: createFileAsync, startAsync, and then.

The first `then` function gets the result. This then passes the result to the handler function. A `BackgroundDownloader` method creates the download operation and `startAsync` creates the routine to initiate the downloads. You can see here that `startAsync` is the one that returns a promise, and we chain it with the second `then()` by returning the value of `startAsync()` in the first completion. The second `then()` is responsible for a completion handler whose parameter contains the download operation.

Example 1B – downloading a web page to a file using startAsync

Another ability to chain the `then()` and `done()` functions is to track the progress of an asynchronous operation by writing a progress function. Due to this, we can not only track the progress but can also obtain a great deal about the error conditions by adding an error function.

In our next example, we will see how to download a web page asynchronously to a file, using the `startAsync` function and with the error handler. The output of this example will be the same as the previous one, but the mechanism will be a bit different:

```
// Allocate the URI where to get the download the file.
var AllocatedUri = new
Windows.Foundation.Uri("http://www.packt.com");

// Get the folder for temporary files.
var temporaryFolder =
Windows.Storage.ApplicationData.current.temporaryFolder;

// Create the temp file asynchronously.
temporaryFolder.createFileAsync("tempfile.txt",
Windows.Storage.CreationCollisionOption.replaceExisting)
  .then(function (tempFile) {

    // lets start the download operation if the createFileAsync
    call succeeded

    var Iamdownloader = new
    Windows.Networking.BackgroundTransfer.BackgroundDownloader();
```

```
    var transfer = Iamdownloader.createDownload(uriExample,
    tempFile);
    return transfer.startAsync();
})
.then(
    //Define the function to use when the download completes
    successfully
    function (result) {
      WinJS.log && WinJS.log("File was download successfully ");
    },

    // this is where we add the error handlers which displays
    function (err) {
      WinJS.log && WinJS.log("File download failed.");
    },
    // Define the progress handling function.
    function (progress) {
      WinJS.log && WinJS.log("Bytes retrieved: " +
      progress.progress.bytesReceived);
    });
```

The only difference in this code is the proper error handler addition, which makes the error handling easy and readable.

Summary

In this chapter, we learned how promises can be implemented in WinRT. We saw how promises evolved in the Windows platform and how it's contributing to different Windows-based devices. We also saw how it helps Windows-based gaming consoles and in the creation of Windows-based apps for Windows Store.

It's the adaptability of promises that has led to it finding its place in all the major leading technologies. Even technology giants such as Microsoft couldn't neglect its existence and are able to give full attention and scope in its present and upcoming technologies.

In the next chapter, we will learn how promises are being implemented in one of the fastest growing server-side JavaScript, the Node.js.

6
Promises in Node.js

In the previous chapter, we learned about promises in WinRT and how they are implemented using the Microsoft platform. The promises concept has had wider coverage than other languages. This is one of the fastest growing concepts in open source technologies.

In this chapter, we will discuss an implementation of JavaScript that is dramatically changing the course of modern web development and enhancing our ways to real-time web. This amazing piece of technology is called Node.js, a platform written in JavaScript and based on the V8 Engine by Google. Promises in Node.js are far more interesting, evolving, and productive than any other platform or implementation can offer. Let's dive into the details and find out what promises in Node.js have to offer for real-time web.

The V8 engine – the mechanics

A term that was only known to Formula One racers and sports car manufacturers was brought into web browsers in 2008 when Google first launched its amazing web browser, Google Chrome.

Like many real-life products and their mechanisms were being copied and depicted in computing industry, the V8 engine is one the true examples of such modeling in recent times. Since the scope of this book is focused on promises, let's take a brief look at what the V8 engine is in reality.

The V8 engine is a nontraditional engine with eight cylinders mounted on a crankshaft to produce extra horsepower. This engine is smoother than a V6 (another V-shaped engine), and less expensive than a V12 engine.

The V8 engine in Google Chrome

An open source project that makes Google number one in the web browser race is Google Chrome. Chrome is built on an exclusively designed JavaScript Engine called the V8. Based on V8, Chrome has gained popularity and attention from users all around the world in a very short space of time. It was first rolled out on September 2, 2008. However, what does this V8 JavaScript engine do which makes it faster and exceptional than any other program? It doesn't go into compiling the high-level language interpreter to machine code. It basically skips the middle part of code interpreting and converts the high-level code to machine code then and there. This is the reason why Chrome is much faster:

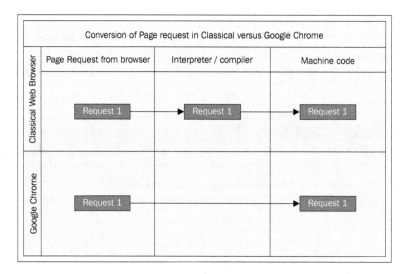

The evolution of Node.js

After the release of Google Chrome as an open source web browser, people started to take interest in it. There were two main reasons for this rapid interest. From a common user's perspective, it was much faster than any other web browser available, and from a developer's perspective, it was something that had revolutionized the browser technology by converting the high-level instructions into machine code instantly, removing a complete layer of middleware of compiler or interpreter.

Many developers started exploring the code base to find the possibilities of solutions they were involved in and to get the most out of this new amazing compilation of codebase.

Ryan Dahl was among those developers who wanted to give a shot to V8 JavaScript engine as he was busy trying to solve a problem while working at Joyent. The problem was making a browser know how much time is left for an upload process. Inspired by the recent release of V8 and Ruby's Mongrel web server, he drafted the codebase that later evolved into Node.js.

A brief introduction to Node.js

What Dahl had created was the first release of a brand new concept in the modern web app development, Node.js.

In plain words, its server-side JavaScript is built on Google's V8 engine. Node.js is an event-based and nonblocking I/O. It's lightweight, efficient, and best suited for data-intensive real-time web apps that run on distributed devices.

Download and install Node.js

You can download Node.js from its official website at `http://nodejs.org/download`.

Node.js is available for a variety of platforms. Select your operating system and the installer will guide you through the rest.

Node.js is also available on GitHub as an open source project at `https://github.com/joyent/node` for developers around the world to contribute to its evolution and development.

The installation instructions are quite simple and easy to understand, just follow the installers related to your operating systems. This is quite straightforward and the process gets completed without much hassle. All you need to do is just follow the onscreen instructions.

Node Package Manager – NPM

One of the best virtues of using Node.js is NPM or Node Package Manager. It's an effective way for developers to collaborate on ideas by sharing codebase in a much faster way. However, this is not it. The best use of NPM is to download and install a different simple directory of code called the **package**. It can be done easily by just typing in simple commands (such as `npm install express`) that will download and install the entire package on your machine. With every package, there is a `.json` file that has the metadata about the package. In Unix-based environments, Node Package Managers not only help in downloading and setting up other packages, but are also able to update Node.js itself.

NPM is also another reason why Node.js is getting popular in the community of JavaScript developers. Unlike other languages where uploading libraries and binaries are very time-consuming and permission-oriented. With NPM, it's a much faster and less-permission oriented model that fascinates developers to upload and share their work throughout the community.

For more information on NPM and to add your contributions, check out `https://www.npmjs.com/`.

In later sections, we will see how NPM will help us in installing and using packages of our choice and how much faster and sleeker it is to work with NPM.

Choice of environment

Node.js is platform independent in a way that it has all the installations, setups, and libraries available for all the major operating systems currently available. It's available for all Unix-based operating systems, as well as Mac and Windows platforms. Since our prime focus here is to make you understand what the link is between Node.js and promises, we will base our code examples on the Windows 7 (any edition) platform since it's widely available and Node.js is also available for Windows 7 in stable conditions. Plus, it's very simple and less time-consuming.

 Please remember that using Windows-based systems won't make any difference to code and their outputs. This will remain the same for every operating system with no change of any kind. You can easily use the same codebase on any other operating system without any hesitation.

Setting up the environment for Node.js

Let's familiarize ourselves with the environment and how things are getting done using Node.js. First things first, we must know how to set up things to compile the code and run it over our machine.

If you are reading this section, it's assumed that you already have Node.js installed on your machine with the latest release; otherwise, please refer to the earlier section to download and install Node.js.

After you have set up Node.js, check which version of Node.js and NPM is available on your machine by typing in the following commands:

```
D:\> node -v
D:\> NPM  -v
```

The output should be similar to the following screenshot:

Checking versions of Node.js and NPM

Please note that the current version of Node.js is 0.10.31 and the current version of NPM is 1.4.23. Our examples will be based on these versions, not lesser than these versions.

A simple node server

Now, we have our environment ready to do some experiments, let's get the most obvious activity done by trying a simple node server. For this, you only need two pieces of software. One is your default text editor such as Notepad in Windows or Nano for Ubuntu and a web browser. For the web browser, we prefer to use Google Chrome as it's easily available for all platforms and is native to Node.js.

So, type the following code in your favorite text editor:

```
// simple server written in Nodejs
// This server would be running on default IP http://127.0.0.1
var http = require('http');
http.createServer(function (request, response)
{
  response.writeHead(200, {'Content-Type': 'text/plain'}); // this
  defines the MIME type of content
```

```
    response.end('Hello World\n'); // this is the browser's output.
}).listen(1337, '127.0.0.1'); // 1337 is the port number where the
browser is listing to this request.
console.log('Server running at http://127.0.0.1:1337/'); //This
line will show at command prompt
```

Save the file by any name with the `.js` extension. For our example, we use the name `server_example.js`. Save this file in a directory (such as `Promises_in_Node`) and open your terminal program. For Windows, it will be Command Prompt. Navigate to the directory where you have saved your file and type in the following command:

```
D:\Promises_in_Node> node server_example.js
```

If the code has no errors, it will compile and show the following output on the screen:

```
D:\Promises_in_Node> node server_example.js
Server running at http://127.0.0.1:1337/
```

Now, open Chrome and type `http://127.0.0.1:1337/` in the address bar and hit *Enter*. This screen will show you the successful output from the Node.js server:

That's it! You are now ready to take a deep dive in to promises in Node.js.

Things we learned so far

Let's sum up what we have learned so far. We learned what V8 engine is and how it's developed by Google Chrome as a JavaScript engine, what Node.js is and how it was started as a problem-solving technique to a full-fledged application development platform. We learned about the Node Package Manager and how it can be used in the Node.js application development. We then learned about where to download Node.js, how to install it, and what dependencies we have to take in consideration while developing for Node.js, and finally, we learned to write a simple server using Node.js and seen its output in a browser. This is a check point and if you are still confused about Node.js, please read through again and then move on.

The following sections will let you understand more about Node.js and promises and how promises are gaining so much respect from Node.js developers.

Node.js with the Q library

In *Chapter 2, The JavaScript Asynchronous Model*, we discussed what callback hell is and how we are dealing with using promises. With every language, implementation also changes. The same case is with Node.js. promises in Node.js are implemented in a different way. In Node.js, promises are not only used for dealing with callback hell, instead if a function cannot return a value or throw an exception, it can easily pass on a promise. This is a little different from what we have seen in the previous chapters. From the perspective of Node.js, a promise is an object that represents the return value or that can throw an exception Furthermore, it can also be used as a proxy for a remote object to improve latency.

Let's have a look at the following code:

```
process_one(function (value1) {
    process_two(value1, function(value2) {
        process_three(value2, function(value3) {
            process_four(value3, function(value4) {
                // Do something with value4
            });
        });
    });
});
```

Messy, isn't it? Not only is it messy, but also very confusing and hard to maintain. Now, look at the following code using promise:

```
Q.fcall(process_one)
.then(process_two)
.then(process_three)
.then(process_four)
.then(function (value4) {
    // Do something with value4
})
.catch(function (error) {
    // Error Handler
})
.done();
```

Now, this code is less confusing, more productive, and it has one additional quality, which is an implicit error propagation like we have try-catch and finally blocks in Java that catch any unwanted exception and save the program from crashing totally when encountered with an unexpected condition.

The callback approach is known as the inversion of control, a function that is capable of accepting a callback rather than returning a value. Such a mechanism can more easily be described as the phrase, *Don't call me, I will call you.*

Promises in Q have a very special tendency as it's clearly made independent the input arguments from control flow arguments. One can only be able to see its true benefits when using and creating APIs, particularly, variadic, rest, and spread arguments.

Moving ahead with Q

After a brief introduction to Node.js and Q, let's see how we can develop applications. First, we need to get the Q library to set up the modules for it.

Using the Node Package Manager, install the Q library as shown in the following screenshot:

```
D:\Promises_in_Node>npm install q
q@1.2.0 node_modules\q

D:\Promises_in_Node>
```

As you can see, the prompt says its q at version 1.2.0, which is stable and also backward compatible. We will use this release for all our examples in this chapter.

With this installation and past upgrades in our environment, we are now able to sample some of the common yet fruitful features that promises give us in Q.

Promises have a then method, which you can use to get the eventual return value (fulfillment) or throw an exception (rejection). By now, we all know it, after reading the previous chapters of this book.

```
iPromiseSomething() .then(function (value) { //your code },
function (reason) { //your code } );
```

Here is how the preceding line of code works:

- If iPromiseSomething returns a promise that gets fulfilled later with a return value, the first function (the fulfillment handler) will be called

- If the iPromiseSomething function gets rejected later by a thrown exception, the second function (the rejection handler) will be called with the exception

As you can see, the resolution of a promise is always asynchronous, which means the fulfillment or rejection handler will always be called in the next turn of the event loop (that is, process.nextTick in Node.js). This mechanism ensures that it will always return a value either before the fulfillment or rejection handlers are executed.

Propagation in Q

The then method always returns a promise that will either be handled or rejected.

In our example code, we assign the output to the reapPromise variable, which will hold the value:

```
var reapPromise  = getInputPromise()
.then(function (input) {
}, function (reason) {
});
```

The reapPromise variable is the new promise for the return value of either handler. Only one handler will ever be called and it will be responsible for resolving reapPromise as a function, which can only either return a value (a future value) or throw an exception.

Whatever is the case, there will be the following possible outcomes:

- If you return a value in a handler, reapPromise will get fulfilled
- If an exception is thrown in a handler, reapPromise will get rejected
- If a promise is returned in a handler, reapPromise will become that promise
- As it will become a new promise, it will be useful for managing delays, combining results, or recovering from errors.

If the getInputPromise() promise gets rejected and you forget the rejection handler, the error will go to reapPromise:

```
var reapPromise = getInputPromise()
.then(function (value) {
});
```

If the input promise gets fulfilled and you fail the fulfillment handler, the value will go to reapPromise:

```
var reapPromise = getInputPromise()
.then(null, function (error) {
});
```

When you are only interested in handling the error, Q promises to provide a fail shorthand:

```
var reapPromise = getInputPromise()
.fail(function (error) {
});
```

If you are writing JavaScript for modern engines only or using CoffeeScript, you may use catch instead of fail.

Promises also provide a `fin` function that is like a `finally` clause. The final handler gets called, with no arguments, when the promise returned by `getInputPromise()` either returns a value or throws an error.

The value returned or error thrown by `getInputPromise()` passes directly to `reapPromise` unless the final handler fails, and may be delayed if the final handler returns a promise:

```
var reapPromise = getInputPromise()
.fin(function () {
});
```

In short:

- If the handler returns a value, the value is ignored
- If the handler throws an error, the error passes to `reapPromise`
- If the handler returns a promise, `reapPromise` gets postponed

The eventual value or error has the same effect as an immediate return value or thrown error; a value would be ignored, an error would be forwarded.

So when we are looking for propagation, we need to keep in mind what we want to see from our returning value. The `then`, `fail`, and `fin` functions are the keys to remember while using propagations in Q.

 If you are writing JavaScript for modern engines, you may use `finally` instead of `fin`.

Chaining and nesting promises

Remember chaining in promises in *Chapter 2, The JavaScript Asynchronous Model*, where we learned all the things about chaining and callback hell handling? This is just same for Node.js using Q.

There are two ways you can chain a promise in Node.js using Q: one is you can chain a promise inside a handler and the other is outside of it.

Let's suppose we are doing multiple things at a time, we can set up the promise chain like this:

```
f1_promise()
    .then(function() { return s1_promise(); })
    .then(function() { return t1_promise();  })
        ...
    .then(function() { return nth_promise();      });
```

So, we can say that the `ANY_promise()` function can contain some behavior, and this will return a promise object that leads to eventually return a result. As soon as the real result is returned, it will set off the next function in the chain.

This looks good now, what if you want to set off an asynchronous function and wait until we get a result before executing the behavior of the next promise in the chain?

Q has a solution for this. Using `.defer()` and `deferred.resolve()`, you can get it in a much more manageable and predictable manner.

Sequences in Q

Like chaining, sequences is another way to stage your result in the way you want. Sequence is the way you can use in a predefined manner to get the outcome of the situation as desired. To hold it more tightly and to generate the result, Q provides sequences in a unique way.

Suppose you have a number of promise-generating functions, all of them need to be run in a sequence. You can do it manually like this example:

```
return seq(startValue).then(secondValue).then(thirdValue);
```

You have to make sure that every `then()` must be in a sequence with another `then();` to maintain the sequence. Failing to do so will break the sequence, and you will not be able to get another value later.

The other way is to instruct your sequence dynamically. This can be faster but needs more attention while executing the code as unpredictable code may harm the overall sequence.

Here is a snippet of how you can do it dynamically:

```
var funcs = [startValue, secondValue, thirdValue];

var result = Q(startValue);
funcs.forEach(function (f) {
    result = result.then(f);
});
return result;
```

If this looks like you are using too many lines of code, use `reduce`:

```
return func.reduce(function (tillNow, f) {
    return tillNow.then(f);
}, Q(startValue));
```

Combination in Q

With Q, you have a unique facility in Node.js to write cleaner and manageable code if you want to combine a list of array of promises. This can help you to write a more complex level of sequential data structure in a more manageable way. How can we get there? Use `all`. Consider the following example:

```
return Q.all([
    eventAdd(2, 2),
    eventAdd (10, 20)
]);
```

The `Q.all([func1(), func2()]);` function will be the generic form of the preceding code. You can also use `spread` to replace `then`. Can we replace another new thing with Q? Not really! The `spread` function spreads the values over the arguments of the fulfillment handler. For the rejection handler, it will get the first signal of failure. So, any of the promises destined to fail first will get it handled by a rejection handler:

```
function eventAdd (var1, var2) {
    return Q.spread([var1, var2], function (var1, var2) {
        return a + b;
    })
```

```
}

Q.spread(). Call all initially

return getUsr() .then(function (userName) { return [username,
getUser(userName)]; }) .spread(function (userName, user) {
});
```

When you call the function, it will return `allSettled`. Within this function, a promise will be returned as an array that holds the value. When this promise has been fulfilled, the array contains the fulfillment values of the original promise within the same sequence as those promises. The beauty is, if any promise is rejected, it will be rejected immediately, not waiting for the rest of others to come and share their statuses:

```
Q.allSettled(promises)
.then(function (results) {
    results.forEach(function (result) {
        if (result.state === "fulfilled") {
            var value = result.value;
        } else {
            var reason = result.reason;
        }
    });
});
```

The `any` function takes in an array of promises to return a promise that is fulfilled by the first given promise to be fulfilled, or rejected, provided all the given promises were rejected:

```
Q.any(promises).then(function (firstPromise) {
    // list of any of the promises that were fulfilled.
}, function (error) {
    // All of the promises were rejected.
});
```

How to handle errors in Q in Node.js

There are times when rejection occurs with the promises creating errors. These errors are clever enough to dodge the handler assigned to take care of such errors. So, we need to take care of them explicitly.

Let's have a look at the following snippet and see how it can be handled:

```
return scenario().then(function (value) {
    throw new Error("I am your error mesg here .");
}, function (error) {
    // We only get here if scenario fails
});
```

Why is this case happening? Suppose the parallelism between promises and try/catch and while we are trying to execute scenario(), the error handler represents a catch for scenario(), while the fulfillment handler represents code that happens after the try/catch block. Now, this code needs its own try/catch block.

The try/catch block is not a new concept for all of you who have written code for some major languages. Since Node.js is based on JavaScript and Q is handling it at the moment, the syntax might be a bit different but the functionality is more or less the same like the following code:

```
Q.
try(function()
    {return scneario().then(function(value)throw new Error("im
    your thrown error");)} )
.catch({ function (error)
    {console.error("i am catched",error)}
});
```

Simply put, in terms of promises, it means you are chaining your rejection handlers.

Making progress with promises

Unlike other libraries, a promise has a unique communication ability. It can update you on its progress if you want it to talk to you. Preferably, these are notifications programmed by developers in a way that it can notify them on specified intervals of time to tell them what is the progress. We can do it by using our favorite then() function:

```
return uploadFile()
.then(function () {
    // Success uploading the file
}, function (err) {
    // There was an error, and we get the reason for error
}, function (progress) {
    // this is where I am reporting back my progress. executed
});
```

There are more than enough advantages of using Q. For this specific topic, it provides us a short call progress which minimizes our effort to only one line using `*.progress();`.

```
return uploadFile().progress(function (progress) {
    // We get notified of the upload's progress
});
```

Getting to the end of a chain of promises

When we are talking about ending a promise chain, we have to make sure that any error doesn't get handled before the end, as it will get rethrown and reported.

This is a temporary solution. We are exploring ways to make unhandled errors visible without any explicit handling.

So, returned like the following code:

```
return hoo()
.then(function () {
    return "foo";
});
Or we can do It like this:
hoo()
.then(function () {
    return "bar";
})
.done();
```

Why are we doing this? Why do we need to invoke the mechanism like this? The answer is very simple, you have to end the chain or have to return it to another promise. This is due to the fact that since handlers catch errors, it's an unfortunate pattern that the exceptions can go unobserved.

Every once in a while, you will need to create a promise from scratch. This is quite normal; you can either create your own promise or get it from another chain. Whatever the case is, consider that it's a beginning. There are a number of ways in which you can create a new promise using Q. Here are some of them:

```
Q.fcall();
//Using this function fcall you can create and  call other //
functions, along with Promise functions. To do that simply //follow
this syntax
return Q.fcall(function () {
    return 10;
});
```

Not only this, `fcall();` can also be used to get an exception-handled promise that looks like the following snippet:

```
return Q.fcall(function () {
    throw new Error("I am an error");
});
```

Since `fcall();` can call functions, or even promised functions, this uses the `eventualAdd();` function to add two numbers:

```
return Q.fcall(eventualAdd, 2, 2);
```

Callback-based promises versus Q-based promises

Say you have to interlink with callback-based instead of promise-based, what would be your options? The answer is Q provides `Q.nfcall()` and `friends();`, but most of the time, we have to rely on `deferred`:

```
var deferred = Q.defer();
FS.readFile("hoo.txt", "utf-8", function (error, text) {
    if (error) {
        deferred.reject(new Error(error));
    } else {
        deferred.resolve(text);
    }
});
return deferred.promise;
```

Normally, we can achieve it like this:

```
//normal way of handling rejected promises.
deferred.reject(new Error("Can't do it"));
//this is how we do it
var rejection = Q.fcall(function () {
    throw new Error("Can't do it");
});
deferred.resolve(rejection);
```

A few words on delay, timeout, and notify

There are situations when we want to make the output of our functions a bit delayed or slower than normal. This is when we are waiting for a certain event to occur such as checking the password's strength at the strength indicator.

For all such needs, Q provides a collection of functions to give you this kind of control. These functions are:

- `Q.delay()`
- `Q.notify()`
- `deferred.notify()`

The preceding functions are not only able to create delays when required but also notify when the delay is likely to occur. If you want to defer the notification, `deferred.notify()` will serve the purpose.

Q.delay()

The following code is a simplified implementation of `Q.delay`:

```
function delay(ms) {
    var deferred = Q.defer();
    setTimeout(deferred.resolve, ms);
    return deferred.promise;
}
```

Q.timeout()

A simple way to work with `Q.timeout`:

```
function timeout(promise, ms) {
    var deferred = Q.defer();
    Q.when(promise, deferred.resolve);
    delay(ms).then(function () {
        deferred.reject(new Error("Timed out"));
    });
    return deferred.promise;
}
```

deferred.notify()

Finally, you can send a progress notification to the promise with
`deferred.notify()`.

There is a wrapper for XML HTTP requests in the browser:

```
function requestOkText(url) {
    var request = new XMLHttpRequest();
    var deferred = Q.defer();
    request.open("GET", url, true);
    request.onload = onload;
    request.onerror = onerror;
    request.onprogress = onprogress;
    request.send();

    function onload() {
        if (request.status === 200) {
            deferred.resolve(request.responseText);
        } else {
            deferred.reject(new Error("Status code was " +
            request.status));
        }
    }

    function onerror() {
        deferred.reject(new Error("Can't XHR " +
        JSON.stringify(url)));
    }

    function onprogress(event) {
        deferred.notify(event.loaded / event.total);
    }

    return deferred.promise;
}
```

Here is an example of how to use this `requestOkText` function:

```
requestOkText("http://localhost:5000")
.then(function (responseText) {
    // If the HTTP response returns 200 OK, log the response text.
    console.log(responseText);
}, function (error) {
    // If there's an error or a non-200 status code, log the
    error.
```

```
        console.error(error);
    }, function (progress) {
        // Log the progress as it comes in.
        console.log("Request progress: " + Math.round(progress * 100)
        + "%");
    });
```

Q.Promise() – another way to create promises

Q.Promise is an alternative promise-creation API that has the same power as the deferred concept, but without introducing another conceptual entity.

Let's rewrite the preceding requestOkText example using Q.Promise:

```
function requestOkText(url) {
    return Q.Promise(function(resolve, reject, notify) {
        var request = new XMLHttpRequest();
        request.open("GET", url, true);
        request.onload = onload;
        request.onerror = onerror;
        request.onprogress = onprogress;
        request.send();

        function onload() {
            if (request.status === 200) {
                resolve(request.responseText);
            } else {
                reject(new Error("Status code was " +
                request.status));
            }
        }
        function onerror() {
            reject(new Error("Can't XHR " + JSON.stringify(url)));
        }
        function onprogress(event) {
            notify(event.loaded / event.total);
        }
    });
}
```

If requestOkText were to throw an exception, the returned promise will be rejected with this thrown exception as the reason for its rejection.

Static methods of Q

Typecasting of promises objects is a must and you must have to convert promises generated from different sources in Q type promises. This is because of the simple fact that not all promise libraries have the same warranties as Q and certainly don't provide all of the same methods.

```
//using when
return Q.when(AmIAvalueOrPromise, function (value) {
}, function (error) {
});
//The following are equivalent:
return Q.all([a, b]);
return Q.fcall(function () {
    return [a, b];
})
.all();
```

Most libraries only provide a partially functional `then` method. Q, on the other hand, is quite different to others:

```
return Q($.ajax(...))
.then(function () {
});
```

If there is any way that the promise you have got is not a Q promise as provided by your library, you should wrap it using a Q function. You can even use `Q.invoke();` as shorthand, as shown in the following code:

```
return Q.invoke($, 'ajax', ...)
.then(function () {
});
```

Promise as a proxy

One marvelous thing about a promise that distinguishes it from the rest is that it can act as a proxy for another object, not only for local objects but also for a remote object. There are methods that let you confidently employ properties or call functions. All of these exchanges return promises, so that they can be chained.

Here is list of functions you can use as proxies of a promise:

Direct manipulation	Using a promise as a proxy
`value.foo`	`promise.get("foo")`
`value.foo = value`	`promise.put("foo", value)`
`delete value.foo`	`promise.del("foo")`
`value.foo(...args)`	`promise.post("foo", [args])`
`value.foo(...args)`	`promise.invoke("foo", ...args)`
`value(...args)`	`promise.fapply([args])`
`value(...args)`	`promise.fcall(...args)`

You can trim round-trips by using these functions instead of `then()` if the promise is a proxy for a remote object.

Even in the case of local objects, these methods can be used as shorthand for particularly-simple gratification handlers. For example, you can replace:

```
return Q.fcall(function () {
    return [{ foo: "bar" }, { foo: "baz" }];
})
.then(function (value) {
    return value[0].foo;
});
```

With the following code:

```
return Q.fcall(function () {
    return [{ foo: "bar" }, { foo: "baz" }];
})
.get(0)
.get("foo");
```

Familiarizing Node.js – the Q way

When you're working with functions that make use of the Node.js callback pattern, where callbacks are in the form of *function(err, result)*, Q provides a few advantageous service functions for adapting between them. The two most important functions are: `Q.nfcall()` and `Q.nfapply()`:

- `Q.nfcall()`: The Node.js function call

  ```
  return Q.nfcall(FS.readFile, "foo.txt", "utf-8");
  ```

- `Q.nfapply()`: The Node.js function apply

```
return Q.nfapply(FS.readFile, ["foo.txt", "utf-8"]);
```

They are both used for calling functions with the same resemblance of Node.js so that they can generate promises.

Unbinds and its solution

When you are working with methods, instead of simple functions, it's highly likely that you can easily run into the common problems where passing a method to another function—such as `Q.nfcall`—unbinds the method from its owner. Q has to offer its services here too so that you can avoid this, by adopting any of these two ways:

- Use `Function.prototype.bind()`
- Use these methods provided by Q:

```
return Q.ninvoke(redisClient, "get", "user:1:id"); // node invoke
return Q.npost(redisClient, "get", ["user:1:id"]); // node post
```

There is yet another way you can create reusable wrappers, using:

- `Q.denodeify`:

```
//using Q.denodeify
var readFile = Q.denodeify(FS.readFile);
return readFile("foo.txt", "utf-8");
```

- `Q.nbind`:

```
// Q.nbind
var redisClientGet = Q.nbind(redisClient.get, redisClient);
return redisClientGet("user:1:id");
```

Q support for tracing stacks

Q also extends its optional support for long stack traces; this helps developers to manage the stack property of an error by providing the entire reasons of errors and rejection reason rather to simply halt without any meaningful or readable error.

The following function is one such example where the error was not handled in a meaningful manner and when someone tried to execute this snippet, he/she experienced meaningless and untraceable errors:

```
function TheDepthOfMyCode() {
```

```
    Q.delay(100).done(function explode() {
        throw new Error("hello I am your error Stack!");
    });
  }
  TheDepthOfMyCode ();
```

This will gives us a raw-looking unhelpful stack trace looking similar to this:

```
Error: hello I am your error Stack!
    at explode (/path/to/test.js5:166)
    at _fulfilled (/path/to/test.js:q:54)
    at resolvedValue.promiseDispatch.done (/path/to/q.js:923:20)
    at makePromise.promise.promiseDispatch (/path/to/q.js:400:23)
    at pending (/path/to/q.js:397:39)
    at process.startup.processNextTick.process._tickCallback (node.
js:244:9)
```

However, if you turn this feature on by setting `Q.longStackSupport = true`, then this will give us a nice-looking helpful stack trace looking similar to this:

```
Error: hello I am your error Stack!
    at explode (/path/to/test.js:3:11)
From previous event:
    at theDepthsOfMyProgram (/path/to/test.js:2:16)
    at Object.<anonymous> (/path/to/test.js:7:1)
```

Unlike most of the time, in JavaScript, we use breakpoints or use `alert()` to see where the error occurred, which is quite frustrating and time consuming. Q has not only given us an elegant way to get to a point where the error is happening, but also the entire trace can be read and analyzed to solve the problem.

In Node.js, this feature can also be enabled through the `Q_DEBUG` environment variable:

> `Q_DEBUG=1 node server.js`

This will enable long stack support at every instance of Q.

Making promise-based actions

Starting off with Q, perform actions that return promises. Let's say, make Node.js action `http.get` as the promised action:

```
// using-promise.js
var httpGet = function (opts) {
    var deferred = Q.defer();
    http.get(opts, deferred.resolve);
    return deferred.promise;
};
```

Later, you can use: `httpGet(...).then(function (res) {...});` but you have to make sure that functions return promises. The first `Q.defer()` returns a set of an empty promise and operations for it. The `deferred.promise` is the empty promise which fixes a certain value:

```
// promise-resolve-then-flow.js
var deferred = Q.defer();
deferred.promise.then(function (obj) {
    console.log(obj);
});


deferred.resolve("Hello World");
```

This prints `Hello World` to the console. In general, you can transform usual callback actions:

```
// promise-translate-action.js
action(arg1, arg2, function (result) {
    doSomething(result);
});
```

To promise actions:

```
// promise-translate-action.js
var promiseAction = function (arg1, arg2) {
    var deferred = Q.defer();
    action(arg1, arg2, deferred.resolve);
    return deferred.promise;
}

promiseAction(arg1, arg2).then(function (result) {
    doSomething(result);
});
```

Object handling promises

We learned a great deal about how promises help object handling whether these are local objects or remote ones. As mentioned earlier, the `then` callback can use the result in any way. Also, each handling is decomposed primitives of property accesses or function calls, for example:

```
// object-unsued.js
httpGet(url.parse("http://abc.org")).then(function (response) {
    return response.headers["location"].replace(/^http:/, "");
}).then(console.log);
```

Decomposition of primitive access

Q can decompose continuous actions of each primitive access. Let's have a look at the following code:

```
// object-decomposed.js
httpGet(url.parse("http://abc.org")).then(function (response) {
    return response.headers;
}).then(function (handlers) {
    return handlers["location"];
}).then(function (location) {
    return location.replace(/^http:/, "");
}).then(console.log);
```

There is another good thing about promises of Q. They have a support method of primitive access as a promise.

By them, the decomposed actions also translate to:

```
// object.primitive.js
httpGet(url.parse("http://example.org"))
    .get("handlers").get("location").post("replace", [/^http:/,
""])
    .then(console.log);
```

View revisited

The `view()` method helps in mirroring all the values into Q-based promises without any distinction, either it comes from a value or any other function. There are two methods that can make this possible:

- `promise.post(name)`
- `promise.send(name)`

This converts a method of the promise value to a promise of the method result.

A result of `view()` has methods for all methods of the promise value. You can use view in the `then` callback of `view()`, for example:

```
// object-view.js
Q.resolve(new Date()).view().then(function (dateView) {
    return dateView.toTimeString().then(function (str) {
        return /\((.*)\)/.exec(str)[0]
    });
}).then(console.log);
```

Aborting a promise

We saw how `done();` is used earlier, but here it comes in with a total impression.

Using `done();`, we can conclude our promise and abort our program. I always have a way to chain the promises:

```
then().then().done();
```

If the promise is vetted (and did not catch the error before), the `done()` function forcibly spawns an uncatchable error (for example, `setTimeout(function () {throw ex;}, 0)`).

On Node.js REPL, run `Q.reject("uncaught").done()`, then exit with an error.

If the error reached to the `done()` function, you can think of it just a programming bug (not an exception state).

Q utilities for Node.js

In this chapter, we came to know that promises are getting more easy to use within Node.js. The following is the set of all major utilities offered by Q for using Node.js:

- `Q.nfapply(fs.readFile, [filename, encoding]).then(console.log);`
- `Q.nfcall(fs.readFile, filename, encoding).then(console.log);`
- `Q.nfbind(fs.readFile)(filename, encoding).then(console.log);`
- `Q.npost(fs, "readFile", [filename, encoding]).then(console.log);`
- `Q.nsend(fs, "readFile", filename, encoding).then(console.log);`

Q has more to offer, but the preceding ones are the best and most used and sensible use of these can help us write a more manageable, cleaner, and dynamically controlled mechanism.

Summary

This chapter was an amazing journey from start to finish, and it has taught us from the very beginning about Node.js. We didn't opt for explaining stuff in computer science terminology, instead we went to the mechanical part of the V8 engine, and from there we saw how real-world objects can be mapped into computing.

We learned what Node.js is, from where this most amazing library started, who built it, and why and how it's helping us create real-time web apps.

Then we moved to Q, the best way to offer promises to Node.js. We saw how we can install Q and then we saw different ways of using Q along with Node.js. We have also achieved our purpose of using Q as a promises implementation of Node.js.

This chapter will encourage you to start working on Node.js, especially on how to take advantage of Q as the library of promises for Node.js.

In the next chapter, we will be looking in-depth in the world of Angular.js and how it got promises implementation.

7
Promises in Angular.js

In the last chapter, we learned about Node.js and its implementations. We also saw how Node.js can be used to amplify the real-time web and how promises can be used to deliver more efficient apps.

In this chapter, we examine another side of promises implementation, promises in Angular.js.

As we go along, we will learn what is Angular.js, why it was created, what benefits it will give us, and lastly, how promises get implemented in Angular.js.

Let's get started with the introduction of Angular.js and how to set it up. Some sample code and working examples will be provided. We will then move to promises in Angular.js.

The evolution of Angular.js

Since the birth of single-page web applications, there have been a number of ways one can write code for such apps. The usage of single-page web apps has been increasing rapidly due to the fact that they are faster, platform independent, and lightweight for all types of devices and auto-adjust to all screen sizes. This is the main reason why engineers want to develop single-page web apps and are more interested in using libraries and frameworks that ease their routine work.

The inception of Angular.js was on the same concept. The core of Angular.js is that it employs the declarative programming concept that states user interfaces should be used to connect software services, while we can use imperative programming to define business logic.

Angular.js's framework extends classical HTML (HTML5) to couple the content together. It uses a two-way data binding technique that is helpful in the automatic synchronization of both model and views. With all these features, Angular.js is independent of DOM, which helps in increased performance and security standards of coupled modules.

The most notable nonfunctional property of Angular.js is the brain that maintains it—Google.

Google is the force behind the development, maintaining, and releasing of different versions of Angular.js.

Angular.js was first released in the year 2009 with the aim of providing client-side **MVC (model view controller)** implementation that can ease both development and testing of applications. Also, it provides a toolset embedded for creating rich Internet applications and tools for modern real-time web applications.

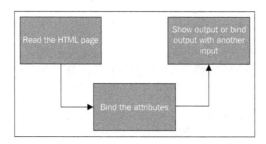

The structure of the Angular.js document

Angular.js uses the HTML file at the base document for its implementation. Its syntax is very simple and easy to remember. The structure of the page is a simple HTML file with ng at its start. This is called the Angular.js directive and it can be used with HTML or can be linked as a individual document.

To start using Angular.js, you need to add a few lines and it will be up and running. For using Angular.js, perform the following steps:

1. Add the ng directive; you only need to add this simple code to start using the Angular.js:

   ```
   <html ng-app="opdsys">
   ```

2. Add the library to the file:

   ```
   <script type="text/JavaScript"
   src="js/lib/angular.min.js"></script>
   ```

3. Now, define the variable within the HTML tag like this:

```
<tr ng-repeat= "reservations in reservation| archive" >
```

4. Finally, you can use it by calling out the variable:

```
<td> {{reservations.id}} < /td>
```

Getting started with Angular.js

To download Angular.js, go to `https://angularjs.org/` and hit the **Download** button. The following dialog box will appear:

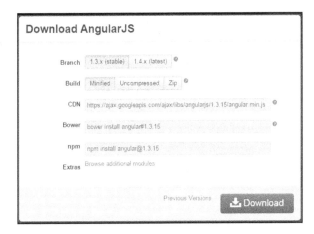

Select the stable and minified build and click on **Download**. This file is a compact one with all the whitespaces removed so that it loads faster. You need to save this file to your working directory as you will need it in the following sections of this chapter.

Creating your first Angular.js file

We will use the downloaded file to include it in our HTML. From there, it will show its magic on how Angular.js is a two-way banded framework and show the results in real time.

Step 1 – create the HTML 5 doc

Create a file like this:

```
<html>
<head>
  <title></title>
```

```
</head>
<body>

</body>
</html>
```

Step 2 – add the JavaScript file to it

Create a JavaScript file with the following code:

```
<html>
<head>
  <title> OPD System</title>
  <script type="text/javascript" src='angular.min.js' ></script>
</head>
<body> </body>
```

Add the Angular.js directive in the preceding code:

```
<html ng-app >
<head>
  <title>OPD System</title>
  <script type="text/javascript" src='angular.min.js' ></script>
</head>
<body>
</body>
```

That's it; you now have a working Angular.js file for further use.

How to use Angular.js on your local machine

There are several ways you can sample Angular.js on your local machine. One way is to use your locally installed server. The XAMPP or Node.js server can be the best option to use for executing the Angular.js code.

You can download the XAMPP server from `https://www.apachefriends.org/download.html` and install it over your PC. Once you are done with installation, you can just drop your Angular.js files/folders in the `htdocs` folder and access these files by simply visiting `http://localhost/source/`, where `source` should be the folder name inside `htdocs`.

Using Node.js, simply paste the following code to a text file and save it as `app.js`:

```
//sample node server from official site at https://nodejs.org/
var http = require('http');
http.createServer(function (req, res) {
  res.writeHead(200, {'Content-Type': 'text/plain'});
  res.end('Hello World\n');
}).listen(1337, '127.0.0.1');
console.log('Server running at http://127.0.0.1:1337/');
```

Save this file to any folder on your drive. Now, open Command Prompt by typing `cmd` in the **Run** utility of your Windows machine and go to the folder where `app.js` is located.

Once you reach there, please type in the following lines and hit **Enter**:

> **node app.js**

You will see the response on screen like this:

Server running at http://127.0.0.1:1337/

Once you get this response, your server is ready to use. Drop your Angular.js files in the same folder where the `app.js` file is located and access it using a browser like this:

http://127.0.0.1:1337/source/

Here, `source` is the folder where `app.js` is located.

What would be your preference for the server?

You can use any of these servers as they both are open source and both have great adoptability for the Angular.js. It's completely up to you which one you can use. To make things more understandable for you, I chose Node.js as it's very handy and easy to maintain with more performance output.

Key elements of Angular.js

Before we get into how promises are implemented in Angular.js, we will first look at the key elements of Angular.js and how they work for us.

Within this section, you will learn the key elements of Angular.js. The skills acquired will be used in the forthcoming sections of this chapter. You will then be able to apply the concepts of promises in Angular.js and write your own custom-made promises in Angular.js as per your need.

The most common elements we will discuss are:

- Supplying scope data
- Filtering output
- Controlling scopes
- Routing views

Supplying scope data

We will play around with the frontend HTML, CSS, and JavaScript to display the results in the browser. We will also get bootstrap from `http://getbootstrap.com/getting-started/#download` to give cosmetic touches in the code:

1. The folder structure must be as defined in the following image. To demonstrate how code works, we will be using the Node.js server. The folder name public needs to deploy at the folder where `app.js` is located. Once the server has started, navigate to `http://127.0.0.1:3000` and you will see the app running there.

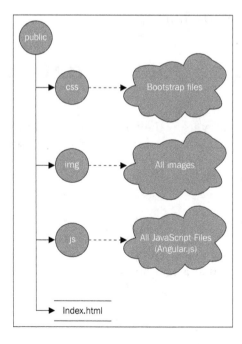

2. We will create an app for available services at a subway station. Let's call this station Stratford from where we will be looking at which subway service is available.

3. Create a file in the `js/controller` folder and name it `app.js`. Here is how this file will look like:

```
function AppCtrl ($scope) {
  $scope.serviceName = {
    "CRTL": {
        "code": "CRTL",
        "name": "Central Line Service",
        "currentLocation": "Oxford Circus",

    },

    "JUBL": {
        "code": "JUBL",
        "name": "Jubblie Line Service",
        "currentLocation": "westham",

    },

    "DLR": {
        "code": "DLR",
        "name": "Docland Ligt railway",
        "currentLocation": " westham",

    },

  };
}
```

4. Now, at the root of the public folder create an HTML file, name it as `index.html`, and add the following code:

```
<html ng-app>
<head>
  <title>Services listing </title>
  <script type="text/javascript"
  src="js/lib/angular.min.js"></script>
  <script type="text/javascript"
  src="js/controllers/app.js"></script>
  <link rel="stylesheet" type="text/css"
  href="css/bootstrap.min.css">
  <link rel="stylesheet" type="text/css" href="css/bootstrap-
  responsive.min.css">
```

```
</head>
<body>
  < ul ng-repeat="services in services">
    <li>{{serviceName.code}}</li>
    <li>{{serviceName.name}}</li>
  </ul> </body>
</html>
```

Now, when you hit refresh at the browser, it will show you which services are away from Stratford station. However, how can this be made possible?

At the top of the HTML doc, there is an ng directive that will create the Angular.js app, and then we can include the JavaScript files; one from Angular.js's minified file and the other is our created JavaScript file that supplies scope to let HTML display it. This all happened due to one variable declaration, $scope.

$scope is responsible for binding data and providing output within the supplied scope. This helps Angular.js to maintain its uniqueness to perform the computation in an isolated or defined area of influence, that's all!

Filtering data

Sometimes, we need to have a specific format of data to display data from our app. Within Angular.js, it's as easy as simply supplying some operators to the element where we want to filter it.

The operator used for this purpose is the pipe, |. As soon as we add a pipe sign, Angular.js knows that we want to filter out something. Let's take a look at two of the most important filters of all:

To convert text in to uppercase at the page output, consider the following code:

```
<html ng-app>
<head>
  <title>Services listing </title>
  <script type="text/javascript"
  src="js/lib/angular.min.js"></script>
  <script type="text/javascript"
  src="js/controllers/app.js"></script>
  <link rel="stylesheet" type="text/css"
  href="css/bootstrap.min.css">
  <link rel="stylesheet" type="text/css" href="css/bootstrap-
  responsive.min.css">
</head>
```

```
<body>
  <div class="container" ng-controller="AppCtrl">
    <h1>Services from Stratford station</h1>
    <ul>
      <li ng-repeat="service in service">{{serviceName.code}}
      - {{serviceName.name | uppercase}}</li>
    </ul>

  </div>
</body>
</html>
```

The most helpful feature of filtering out data is to get an entire object as JSON. This will not only help in the debugging mode, but it's also used to validate the supplied data to see if the format is correct.

Consider the following code which will not only filter out data as a JSON object, but also validate it before displaying the output:

```
<html ng-app>
<head>
  <title>Services listing </title>
  <script type="text/javascript"
  src="js/lib/angular.min.js"></script>
  <script type="text/javascript"
  src="js/controllers/app.js"></script>
  <link rel="stylesheet" type="text/css"
  href="css/bootstrap.min.css">
  <link rel="stylesheet" type="text/css" href="css/bootstrap-
  responsive.min.css">
</head>
<body>
  <div class="container" ng-controller="AppCtrl">
    <h1>Services from Stratford station</h1>
    <ul>
      <li ng-repeat="service in service">{{serviceName.code}}
      - {{serviceName | json}}</li>
    </ul>

  </div>
</body>
</html>
```

This will return the entire JavaScript object as JSON. You can now validate data or get into the debugging mode by getting your hands dirty, digging the JavaScript code and adding `alert()`.

Controlling scopes

We can also supply an entire function to a particular stream instead of a single variable; this will help us interlink the different parts of any app without much hassle. Consider the following JavaScript code which is displaying how we are supplying an entire function to a particular stream:

```javascript
function AppCtrl ($scope) {
  $scope.serviceName = {
    "CRTL": {
      "code": "CRTL",
      "name": "Central Line Service",
      "currentLocation": "Oxford Circus",

    },

    "JUBL": {
      "code": "JUBL",
      "name": "Jubblie Line Service",
      "currentLocation": "westham",

    },

    "DLR": {
      "code": "DLR",
      "name": "Docland Ligt railway",
      "currentLocation": " westham",

    },

  };

  $scope.curretStation = null;

  $scope.setAirport = function (code) {
    $scope.curretStation = $scope.service[code];
  };
}
```

In the last three lines, we added a function that will be fully passed on to the calling ng directive at the HTML output. The code of HTML will look like this:

```
<html ng-app>
<head>
  <title>Services listing </title>
  <script type="text/javascript"
  src="js/lib/angular.min.js"></script>
  <script type="text/javascript"
  src="js/controllers/app.js"></script>
  <link rel="stylesheet" type="text/css"
  href="css/bootstrap.min.css">
  <link rel="stylesheet" type="text/css" href="css/bootstrap-
  responsive.min.css">
</head>
<body>
  <div class="container" ng-controller="AppCtrl">
    <h1>Services from Stratford station</h1>
    <ul>
      <li ng-repeat="Services in ServicesName">
        <a href="" ng-
        click="setAirport(Services.code)">{{Services.code}} -
        {{Services.code}}</a>
      </li>
    </ul>

    <p ng-show="currentStation">Current Services:
    {{currentStationname}}</p>
  </div>
</body>
</html>
```

Notice that we are writing very neat code with very few updates. We can achieve many changes as desired in the last lines before the body tag is completed; you will notice how we have passed an entire function using Angular.js.

Routing views

Conventional websites were made up of many pages linked together via an `href` tag. Their content was hard to read and required more maintenance than ever. With the emergence of single page web apps, the information appeared on the browser instantly as the views can be routed from one link to another without hitting the server repeatedly, or without having to wait for the page to load.

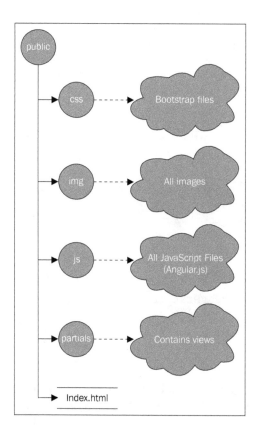

From our examples, we will add another file as a module and place it under the root of the JS folder. The code will look like this:

```
angular.module('services', [])
  .config(airlineRouter);

function airlineRouter ($routeProvider) {
  $routeProvider
    .when('/', {templateUrl: 'partials/destinations.html',
```

```
      controller: 'DestinationsCtrl'})
   .when('/Services/:airportCode', {
     templateUrl: 'partials/stations.html',
     controller: 'ServiceCtrl'
   })
   .when('/service', {
     template: '<h3>Flights</h3> {{Services | json}}',
     controller: 'FlightsCtrl'})
   .when('/reservations', {
     template: '<h3>Your Reservations</h3> {{Services | json}}',
     controller: 'ReservationsCtrl'});
}
```

This will generate views dynamically on the fly at the browser without hitting the server. We need a couple of more files to add more dynamicity. We will add the partials folder in which we placed two more files named services and destination.

The destination.html file will look like this:

```
<div class="pull-left span6">
  <h3>All Destinations</h3>
  <ul>
    <li ng-repeat="destinationin destinations">
      <a href="" ng-click="setDestinations
      (service.code)">{{name.code}} - {{destination.name}}</a>
    </li>
  </ul>

</div>
<div class="span5" ng-include src="sidebarURL"></div>
```

The services.html file will look like this:

```
<div ng-show="CurrentServices">
  <h3>{{CurrentServices.name}}</h3>

  <h4>Destinations</h4>

  <ul>
    <li ng-repeat="destination in CurrentServices.destinations">
      <a ng-href="#/airports/{{destination}}">{{destination}}</a>
    </li>
  </ul>
</div>
```

After editing the `index.html` file at the root of the public folder, the view will look like this:

```html
<html ng-app="ServiceCtrl">
<head>
  <title>Demo</title>
  <script type="text/javascript"
  src="js/lib/angular.min.js"></script>
  <script type="text/javascript"
  src="js/controllers/app.js"></script>
  <script type="text/javascript"
  src="js/controllers/destinations.js"></script>
  <script type="text/javascript"
  src="js/controllers/services.js"></script>
  <script type="text/javascript"
  src="js/controllers/reservations.js"></script>
  <script type="text/javascript"
  src="js/controllers/station.js"></script>
  <script type="text/javascript" src="js/app.js"></script>
  <link rel="stylesheet" type="text/css"
  href="css/bootstrap.min.css">
  <link rel="stylesheet" type="text/css" href="css/bootstrap-
  responsive.min.css">
</head>
<body>
  <div class="container" ng-controller="AppCtrl">
    <h1>AngulAir</h1>

    <ul class="nav nav-pills">
      <li ng-class="destinationsActive">
        <a href="#">Destinations</a>
      </li>
      <li ng-class="servicesActive">
        <a href="#/services">services</a>
      </li>
      <li ng-class="reservationsActive">
        <a href="#/reservations">Reservations</a>
      </li>
    </ul>

    <div ng-view></div>
  </div>
</body>
</html>
```

Implementing promises in Angular.js

Promise is all about how async behavior can be applied on a certain part of an application or on the whole. There is a list of many other JavaScript libraries where the concept of promises exists but in Angular.js, it's present in a much more efficient way than any other client-side applications.

Promises comes in two flavors in Angular.js, one is $q and the other is Q. What is the difference between them? We will explore it in detail in the following sections. For now, we will look at what promise means to Angular.js.

There are many possible ways to implement promises in Angular.js. The most common one is to use the $q parameter, which is inspired by Chris Kowal's Q library. Mainly, Angular.js uses this to provide asynchronous methods' implementations.

With Angular.js, the sequence of services is top to bottom starting with $q, which is considered as the top class; within it, many other subclasses are embedded, for example, $q.reject() or $q.resolve(). Everything that is related to promises in Angular.js must follow the $q parameters.

Starting with the $q.when() method, it seems like it creates a method immediately rather it only normalizes the value that may or may not create the promise object. The usage of $q.when() is based on the value supplied to it. If the value provided is a promise, $q.when() will do its job and if it's not, a promise value, $q.when() will create it.

The schematics of using promises in Angular.js

Since Chris Kowal's Q library is the global provider and inspiration of promises callback returns, Angular.js also uses it for its promise implementations. Many of Angular.js services are by nature promise oriented in return type by default. This includes $interval, $http, and $timeout. However, there is a proper mechanism of using promises in Angular.js. Look at the following code and see how promises maps itself within Angular.js:

```
var promise = AngularjsBackground();
promise.then(
  function(response) {
    // promise process
  },
  function(error) {
```

```
       // error reporting
     },
     function(progress) {
       // send progress

});
```

All of the mentioned services in Angular.js return a single object of promise. They might be different in taking parameters in, but in return all of them respond back in a single promise object with multiple keys. For example, `$http.get` returns a single object when you supply four parameters named `data`, `status`, `header`, and `config`.

```
$http.get('/api/tv/serials/sherlockHolmes ')
  .success(function(data, status, headers, config) {
     $scope.movieContent = data;
});
```

If we employ the promises concept here, the same code will be rewritten as:

```
var promise = $http.get('/api/tv/serials/sherlockHolmes ')
promise.then(
  function(payload) {
     $scope.serialContent = payload.data;
});
```

The preceding code is more concise and easier to maintain than the one before this, which makes the usage of Angular.js more adaptable to the engineers using it.

Promise as a handle for callback

The implementation of promise in Angular.js defines your use of promise as a callback handle. The implementations not only define how to use promise for Angular.js, but also what steps one should take to make the services as "promise-return". This states that you do something asynchronously, and once your said job is completed, you have to trigger the `then()` service to either conclude your task or to pass it to another `then()` method: `/asynchronous _task.then().then().done()`.

In simpler form, you can do this to achieve the concept of promise as a handle for call backs:

```
angular.module('TVSerialApp', [])
  .controller('GetSerialsCtrl',
     function($log, $scope, TeleService) {
       $scope.getserialListing = function(serial) {
         var promise =
```

```
      TeleService.getserial('SherlockHolmes');
    promise.then(
      function(payload) {
        $scope.listingData = payload.data;
      },
      function(errorPayload) {
        $log.error('failure loading serial', errorPayload);
      });
    };
  })
  .factory('TeleService', function($http) {
    return {

      getserial: function(id) {
        return $http.get(''/api/tv/serials/sherlockHolmes' + id);
      }
    }
  });
```

Blindly passing arguments and nested promises

Whatever service of promise you use, you must be very sure of what you are passing and how this can affect the overall working of your promise function. Blindly passing arguments can cause confusion for the controller as it has to deal with its own results too while handling other requests. Say we are dealing with the $http.get service and you blindly pass too much of load to it. Since it has to deal with its own results too in parallel, it might get confused, which may result in callback hell. However, if you want to post-process the result instead, you have to deal with an additional parameter called $http.error. In this way, the controller doesn't have to deal with its own result, and calls such as 404 and redirects will be saved.

You can also redo the preceding scenario by building your own promise and bringing back the result of your choice with the payload that you want with the following code:

```
factory('TVSerialApp', function($http, $log, $q) {
  return {
    getSerial: function(serial) {
      var deferred = $q.defer();
      $http.get('/api/tv/serials/sherlockHolmes' + serial)
        .success(function(data) {
          deferred.resolve({
```

```
                title: data.title,
                cost: data.price});
        }).error(function(msg, code) {
            deferred.reject(msg);
            $log.error(msg, code);
        });
        return deferred.promise;
    }
  }
});
```

By building a custom promise, you have many advents. You can control inputs and output calls, log the error messages, transform the inputs into desired outputs, and share the status by using the deferred.notify(mesg) method.

Deferred objects or composed promises

Since custom promise in Angular.js can be hard to handle sometimes and can fall into malfunction in the worse case, the promise provides another way to implement itself. It asks you to transform your response within a then method and returns a transformed result to the calling method in an autonomous way. Considering the same code we used in the previous section:

```
this.getSerial = function(serial) {
    return $http.get('/api/tv/serials/sherlockHolmes'+ serial)
        .then(
                function (response) {
                    return {
                        title: response.data.title,
                        cost:  response.data.price

                    });
                });
};
```

The output we yield from the preceding method will be a chained, promised, and transformed. You can again reuse the output for another output, chain it to another promise, or simply display the result.

The controller can then be transformed into the following lines of code:

```
$scope.getSerial = function(serial) {
  service.getSerial(serial)
   .then(function(serialData) {
```

```
    $scope.serialData = serialData;
  });
};
```

This has significantly reduced the lines of code. Also, this helps us in maintaining the service level since the automechanism of failsafe in `then()` will help it to be transformed into failed promise and will keep the rest of the code intact.

Dealing with the nested calls

While using internal return values in the `success` function, promise code can sense that you are missing one most obvious thing: the error controller. The missing error can cause your code to stand still or get into a catastrophe from which it might not recover. If you want to overcome this, simply throw the errors. How? See the following code:

```
this.getserial = function(serial) {
    return $http.get('/api/tv/serials/sherlockHolmes' + serial)
        .then(
            function (response) {
                return {
                    title: response.data.title,
                    cost:  response.data.price
                });
            },
            function (httpError) {
                // translate the error
                throw httpError.status + " : " +
                    httpError.data;
            });
};
```

Now, whenever the code enters into an error-like situation, it will return a single string, not a bunch of `$http` statutes or config details. This can also save your entire code from going into a standstill mode and help you in debugging. Also, if you attached log services, you can pinpoint the location that causes the error.

Concurrency in Angular.js

We all want to achieve maximum output at a single slot of time by asking multiple services to invoke and get results from them. Angular.js provides this functionality via its `$q.all` service; you can invoke many services at a time and if you want to join all/ any of them, you just need `then()` to get them together in the sequence you want.

Let's get the payload of the array first:

```
[
    { url: 'myUr1.html' },
    { url: 'myUr2.html' },
    { url: 'myUr3.html' }
]
```

And now this array will be used by the following code:

```
service('asyncService', function($http, $q) {
    return {
        getDataFrmUrls: function(urls) {
            var deferred = $q.defer();
            var collectCalls = [];
            angular.forEach(urls, function(url) {
                collectCalls.push($http.get(url.url));
            });

            $q.all(collectCalls)
            .then(
                function(results) {
                    deferred.resolve(
                        JSON.stringify(results))
                },
                function(errors) {
                    deferred.reject(errors);
                },
                function(updates) {
                    deferred.update(updates);
                });
            return deferred.promise;
        }
    };
});
```

A promise is created by executing `$http.get` for each URL and is added to an array. The `$q.all` function takes the input of an array of promises, which will then process all results into a single promise containing an object with each answer. This will get converted in JSON and passed on to the caller function.

The result might be like this:

```
[
    promiseOneResultPayload,
```

```
    promiseTwoResultPayload,
    promiseThreeResultPayload
]
```

The combination of success and error

The `$http` returns a promise; you can define its success or error depending on this promise. Many think that these functions are a standard part of promise—but in reality, they are not as they seem to be.

Using promise means you are calling `then()`. It takes two parameters—a callback function for success and a callback function for failure.

Imagine this code:

```
$http.get("/api/tv/serials/sherlockHolmes")
.success(function(name) {
    console.log("The tele serial name is : " + name);
})
.error(function(response, status) {
    console.log("Request failed " + response + " status code: " +
    status);
};
```

This can be rewritten as:

```
$http.get("/api/tv/serials/sherlockHolmes")
.success(function(name) {
    console.log("The tele serial name is : " + name);
})
.error(function(response, status) {
    console.log("Request failed " + response + " status code: " +
    status);
};

$http.get("/api/tv/serials/sherlockHolmes")
.then(function(response) {
    console.log("The tele serial name is :" + response.data);
}, function(result) {
    console.log("Request failed : " + result);
};
```

One can use either the `success` or `error` function depending on the choice of a situation, but there is a benefit in using `$http`—it's convenient. The `error` function provides response and status, and the `success` function provides the response data.

This is not considered as a standard part of a promise. Anyone can add their own versions of these functions to promises, as shown in the following code:

```
//my own created promise of success function

promise.success = function(fn) {
    promise.then(function(res) {
        fn(res.data, res.status, res.headers, config);
    });
    return promise;
};

//my own created promise of error function

promise.error = function(fn) {
    promise.then(null, function(res) {
        fn(res.data, res.status, res.headers, config);
    });
    return promise;
};
```

The safe approach

So the real matter of discussion is what to use with $http? Success or error? Keep in mind that there is no standard way of writing promise; we have to look at many possibilities.

If you change your code so that your promise is not returned from $http, when we load data from a cache, your code will break if you expect success or error to be there.

So, the best way is to use then whenever possible. This will not only generalize the overall approach of writing promise, but also reduce the prediction element from your code.

Route your promise

Angular.js has the best feature to route your promise. This feature is helpful when you are dealing with more than one promise at a time. Here is how you can achieve routing through the following code:

```
$routeProvider
    .when('/api/', {
        templateUrl: 'index.php',
```

```
        controller: 'IndexController'
    })
    .when('/video/', {
        templateUrl: 'movies.php',
        controller: 'moviesController'
    })
```

As you can observe, we have two routes: the api route takes us to the index page, with IndexController, and the video route takes us to the movie's page.

```
app.controller('moviesController', function($scope, MovieService) {
    $scope.name = null;

    MovieService.getName().then(function(name) {
        $scope.name = name;
    });
});
```

There is a problem, until the MovieService class gets the name from the backend, the name is null. This means if our view binds to the name, first it's empty, then its set.

This is where router comes in. Router resolves the problem of setting the name as null. Here's how we can do it:

```
var getName = function(MovieService) {
        return MovieService.getName();
    };

$routeProvider
    .when('/api/', {
        templateUrl: 'index.php',
        controller: 'IndexController'
    })
    .when('/video/', {
        templateUrl: 'movies.php',
        controller: 'moviesController'
    })
```

After adding the resolve, we can revisit our code for a controller:

```
app.controller('MovieController', function($scope, getName) {

    $scope.name = name;

});
```

You can also define multiple resolves for the route of your promises to get the best possible output:

```
$routeProvider
  .when('/video', {
      templateUrl: '/MovieService.php',
      controller: 'MovieServiceController',

      // adding one resole here
      resolve: {
          name: getName,
          MovieService: getMovieService,
          anythingElse: getSomeThing
      }
      // adding another resole here
       resolve: {
          name: getName,
          MovieService: getMovieService,
          someThing: getMoreSomeThing
      }
  })
```

Summary

In this chapter, we learned how promise is implemented in Angular.js, how it evolved, and how promises help in creating applications composed for real-time web apps. We also saw the functionality of the Q library and Angular.js implementation of promises using code and learned how to use them in our next application.

The specification of promise in Angular.js is very close to the proposed specification by ECMAScript 6, but there might be a change when Angular.js fully adopts promises as its own specification. It will define its own set of rules to use promise, which might not be the same as the specification itself.

In the next chapter, we will look at how promises are implemented in jQuery, what will be the mechanism, and what benefits it will bring.

8
Promises in jQuery

In the last chapter, we learned how promises were implemented in Angular.js and how they provided benefit in the fast growing real-time web app industry. In this chapter, we will explore another very famous and useful JavaScript library for frontend web/mobile apps development.

jQuery is one the most used JavaScript libraries and it is recognized as one of the most maintainable, progressive, and easy to adopt libraries around. jQuery has also a credit to shrink the mile-long lines of code into plainer and simpler short code. This utility helped jQuery gain popularity beyond imagination. In this chapter, we will be looking at the history of jQuery, how it evolved, what is the basic way to use it, and how promises are playing a part in the maturity of jQuery. Let's start with the history of jQuery in brief.

From where it started?

The classical way of writing code in JavaScript was quite a tedious task. Since the language did not have many set rules, the code written in JavaScript was becoming unattainable and rewriteable. The way developers chose the names of their functions and variables was making simple functions nonreadable and thus not worthy to use in another project of a similar nature. Also, the fact was that JavaScript was considered as a second rated language in the computing world due to which not many people were using it seriously.

In August 2006 the birth of jQuery, enlightened the JavaScript world. John Resig, the brain behind jQuery, announced in his blog post that jQuery 1.0 was released. This was the first time when people really started taking JavaScript seriously and were convinced of its trustworthiness. Though JavaScript has been around since the early 90s (as described in the first chapter), it has seen many ups and downs. Finally, with the release of Firefox browser and jQuery, JavaScript managed to gain some credibility.

Behind the scenes – how does jQuery work?

jQuery is based on a simple line of write less, do more; within a few lines of jQuery code, you will be able to achieve more tasks than conventional ways of writing code. jQuery has made many tasks easy to conclude in a short time span. It also brings neatness and readability in code, which earlier, was rare in JavaScript.

After the arrival of jQuery, things started to change dramatically for JavaScript. Many new implementations started to come on the screen with much more mature approaches, but the place jQuery has gained was unmatched then and still is.

Having said this, let's come back to our topic: how does jQuery work behind the scenes?

It all rotates around the $ sign. The jQuery library provides the jQuery (); function, which allows you select elements just like CSS selectors. For example:

```
var itemsList = jQuery query("ul");
```

Or:

```
var itemsList = $("ul");
```

In the preceding line, the $ sign is the representation of jQuery. In JavaScript, the variable name can be anything, but must not start with a numeric value and must not include a hyphen. In this way, using $ is more convenient for the rules and easy to remember. You may also find functions like this:

```
window.jQuery = window.$ = jQuery;
```

Here the $ sign comes at the very end of the function, and this is the same sight you will notice in the jQuery source code.

The mechanism is when you call $() and supply a selector to it, you are actually creating a new jQuery object. In JavaScript, functions are objects too, which means $() has not only embedded a single object, but it may contain methods, variables, and multiple objects. So, you might use $.support for information on the current environment or you may also use $.ajax for an AJAX call to make an AJAX request.

Is your document ready to submit?

Sometimes, it can happen that you submit your document when its half finished without knowing that it still needs to be processed further. Such an event triggers a chain of events that will eventually make your page or app go into the service-fail mode.

Using jQuery, this is something that happens rarely as it provides the `$(document).ready()` method, which will help to complete of the processing the document. A simple example can be seen here:

```
$(document).ready(function() {
   console.log('ready!');
});
```

The function will execute and will be passed to `.ready()` once the document is ready. We are using `$(document)` to create a jQuery object from the page's document. We will then call the `.ready()` function on that object, passing it the function we want to execute.

How to use jQuery

As we saw in *Chapter 7, Promises in Angular.js*, the documents related to Angular.js was the JavaScript file that was linked in HTML pages to call the functions; the same structure is used in jQuery.

jQuery is a JavaScript file that was linked in at the very beginning of our HTML file. This can be done in two ways: either call the file from its location on the Web or download the JavaScript file on your local hard drive and then embed the code. Either way it will work, but we prefer to use it from our hard drive.

The following lines of code show when we want to link a file from its remote location:

```
<head>
<script src="http://ajax.aspnetcdn.com/ajax/jQuery/
jquery-1.9.min.js"></script>
</head>
```

Or, we can download the file on our local hard drive and change the syntax like this:

```
<head>
<script src="js/jQuery/jquery-1.9.min.js"></script>
</head>
```

Here, `src="js` is indicating the local folder where JavaScript file exists.

In a nutshell, you can either use the already written jQuery by embedding it at the head of the HTML file using the URL or you can download it and make your own modifications. In both ways, your output will be generated on the screen of the browser.

The syntax

The real power of jQuery lies in its custom made syntax, which will help in selecting HTML elements and perform some action. Its syntax is quite straightforward and easy to remember, plus it's very neatly written. Here is a sample of jQuery syntax:

```
$(selector).action ()
```

The dollar sign ($) defines whether you will use jQuery, whereas the `selector` query is to find the HTML element and `action` defines what kind of action will be performed on selected elements.

Here are some examples that will explain how jQuery works using its syntax:

- `$(this).hide()`: This hides the current element
- `$("p").hide()`: The hides all `<p>` elements
- `$(".test").hide()`: This hides all elements with `class="test"`
- `$("#test").hide()`: This hides the element with `id="test"`

These are a few examples of hundreds of other methods provided by jQuery. For the complete reference on methods and APIs, here's the link for all your jQuery needs: `https://api.jquery.com/`.

Caching in jQuery

Let's discuss caching in brief specifically relating to jQuery and as a concept in general.

The concept of caching is as old as the Internet itself, at least with the modern day Internet. Developers are using it to store repetitive data and to reduce cost to server calls or to remember the connection between the user and server.

Caching helps in many ways to boost the performance of web apps by writing images and sending the session's information to the user's hard drive at a special location called the temporary storage. Mostly, this location is specifically created on the local hard drive and is there to deal with such type of data.

Say you are surfing an online shopping cart over your browser. At the very first instance, the site is being loaded to your temporary memory. This includes adding images of products and other meta information that marks the initial caching of that particular website. Now, say you have decided to purchase a product and signed in to the user's area of the shopping cart. This will cache your information in a little text file called a cookie, which holds the information about who you are and remembers the web server you are talking to. This is a flow of caching your information over the temporary location to reduce server calls, optimize navigation, and let the server remember your identity.

What does jQuery have to offer when it comes to caching and handing elements that need to cache? Let's take a look.

Caching in jQuery is offered by data function, and it's the same as any other function calls you make within jQuery. This function itself allows you to bind random data to random selectors. Most of the developers use it for manipulation with DOM elements, but this is not limited to it. You can add multiple selectors to bind to multiple references at a given time slot as the function takes care of it automatically; it's as simple and easy as this. However, how do the elements and their handlers stay in the memory?

jQuery follows the "name corresponds value" method to write and handle the elements in the memory. The unique part of it is the name of element can be same for many entries, but they must have to point to different DOM elements. In this way, reference by value comes into play and referring to a particular element will be faster and easy to traverse by the program using it.

Now, to add elements to the data function, we will follow a syntax similar to the one shown here:

```
$("#Textbox_").data("im_textbox1", value)
```

From here, you can see that we bind the selector with the `data()` function, and within the function, we supplied two parameters as the name and its corresponding value. In this way, we can bind as many selectors as we want to cache them up.

However, the story has a twist. You can write in cache using `data()`, but it won't remove data on its own. You have to remove it manually from the temporary memory. You can do it by calling out the `removeData()` method like this:

```
$("#Textbox_").removeData(value)
```

Of course, you can automate the function call of `removeData()` by writing some kind of cron/timer job function. However, this requires smart engineering and loads of dry run to that particular job as this can wipe out any important data from the temporary storage permanently, so it's advised to use such timer jobs in a very careful manner.

Overall, caching in jQuery is an essential component, and without this, you cannot optimize your application's flow and data traversing. Using jQuery cache will also optimize the number of server calls and will boost the performance of your piece of code.

A sample example

Before we start the prime topic of this chapter, we need to understand how we draft files that can use jQuery query. This will give us a better understanding of the code level working and will make us skilled to use promises in jQuery.

Let's start with selectors.

Selectors

Selectors enable us to select and manipulate HTML. We can use them to find HTML elements that are based on their IDs: classes, types, attributes, values, and much more stuff. These selectors are just like selectors in CSS, but with the jQuery touch. Here touch is all the selectors start with the dollar sign, $, followed by round brackets and dot, as shown in the following code:

```html
<!DOCTYPE html>
<html>
    <head>
        <title> Selector in action </title>
        <script src="http://code.jquery.com/jquery-
        1.9.0.js"></script>
        <script>
          $(document).ready(function(){
              $("button").click(function(){
                  $("p").hide(); // this will able to select
                  paragraph element from HTML
              });
          });
        </script>
    </head>
    <body>
```

```
    <h2>I am a heading </h2> <!-- this is the place from where
    the  paragraph is selected -->
    <p>I am a paragraph.</p>
    <button>I am a button </button>
    </body>
</html>
```

Have a look at the preceding code. The script tag right after the `</script>` tag is the place where the selector defines itself and then processes the requests. Once the page is loaded, it will say "I am a paragraph" with a button, and when you click on it, the name of the button will change to "I am a button" from "I am a paragraph." This all happened without any page change since jQuery was able to play with HTML elements on the go and display results on the same page. This is one helpful feature of jQuery out of the many that developers are using on a daily basis. Such binding, instantaneous computing is the reason why jQuery is the choice of many groups of developers.

Event methods

jQuery has many event-driven interfaces. These interfaces are invoked when you trigger some event. There are many events such as mouse click, double-click by mouse, keystroke, mouse hover, and touch. They are made simple by jQuery; all you need to do is write a few lines of code and the rest of the processing will be taken over by the jQuery library. Have a look at the following example:

```
<!DOCTYPE html>
<html>
    <head>
        <script src="http://code.jquery.com/jquery-
        1.9.0.js"></script>
        <script>
            $(document).ready(function(){
                $("h1").click(function(){
                    $(this).hide();
                });
            });
        </script>
    </head>
    <body>
        <h1> Click me to make me disappear </h1>
    </body>
</html>
```

Okay, what will happen to the page when I click on the text that appears on the screen? Any guesses? Yes, it will disappear as I passed the value of the h1 tag into the jQuery function, which will then hide it when it senses the mouse has been clicked on it. This is how we normally used to play around with placeholders in the forms or text areas, but nowadays, forms have this ability built in.

Having said this, it's time to move on to the core of our chapter.

JavaScript before and after jQuery

There was a time when a simple mouse click can be caught by a simple function, element.onClick = functionName. This was good till the time another function came about that wanted to listen to the same click. This was solved by adding the addListenerEvent function from the DOM function. This had added as many possible listener functions, and we used to adopt this approach.

However, such happenings are meant to reoccur as we are now facing the same problem with AJAX calls. AJAX uses a single callback function and not only the jQuery $ajax(), but also the XMLHttpRequest object which has similar problems.

The solution – introducing promises in jQuery

The solution to the preceding problem was finally delivered in jQuery 1.5 as the deferred object. Before the deferred concept was introduced in jQuery, the typical AJAX call was something like this:

```
$.ajax({
  url: "/testURL.com",
  Success: TheSuccessFunction,
  Error: TheErrorFunction
});
```

Can you guess what could be the output of this function? Yes, a single XMLHttpRequest object, which is quite expected for those who are still maintaining the apps built before jQuery 1.5.

Now, what dramatical change was introduced in jQuery 1.5. First of all, it's based on a specification of common JavaScript that defines common interfaces and can be extended as per the needs, and secondly, they are quite global and you can use these in similar services, such as Node.js.

After the addition of deferred objects in jQuery 1.5, the preceding code was rewritten like this:

```
var promise = $.ajax({
  url: "/testURL.com"
});
promise.done(TheSuccessFunction);
promise.fail(TheErrorFunction);
```

If you want to write a more concise version of the preceding code, it can be achieved as follows:

```
var promise = $.ajax({
  url: "/testURL.com"
});

promise.then(TheSuccessFunction,TheErrorFunction);
```

Likewise, there are a number of other advancements that were brought in by introducing promise in jQuery. In the following sections, we will take a closer look into how jQuery is getting its promises fulfilled.

Deferred in jQuery

Like in any other implementation of promises, `Deferred` also has its importance and value in jQuery. The power lies in the implementation of the concept, which is straightforward, yet very powerful. In jQuery, `deferred` has two important methods that are used to attach with three important events so that they can be linked to a callback. The methods are `resolve` and `reject`, and the events that can be attached with a callback are `done()`, `fail()`, and `always()`. Let's see it with an example:

```
<!DOCTYPE html>
<html>
  <head>
    <script src="http://code.jquery.com/jquery-
    1.9.0.js"></script>
    <script>
      var deferred = $.Deferred();

      deferred.done(function(value) {
      alert(value);
      });
```

```
            deferred.resolve("hello $.deferred ");

        </script>
    </head>
    <body>
        <h1> $.deferred was just displayed </h1>
    </body>
</html>
```

The thing to remember here is that callback will always be executed no matter whether deferred is resolved or not, but when you call the reject method, the failed callback will be executed. Having said that, our preceding example can look like this:

```
<!DOCTYPE html>
<html>
    <head>
        <script src="http://code.jquery.com/jquery-
        1.9.0.js"></script>
        <script>
            var deferred = $.Deferred();

            deferred.resolve("hello resolve");

            deferred.done(function(value) {
                alert(value);
            });

        </script>
    </head>
    <body>
        <h1> sample example of Deferred  object.  </h1>
    </body>
</html>
```

If we are to summarize what the $.Deferred object is; we can say it's just a promise that has methods, which will allow its owner to either resolve or reject it.

$.Deferred().promise() in jQuery

One of the shiny stars of Deferred is its promises. What this method can do? Well, it returns an object, and with nearly the same interface as Deferred. However, there is a catch. It's there just to attach the callbacks and not to resolve or reject.

This is quite useful in some other conditions, say you want to call out an API. This will not have the ability to resolve or reject the deferred. Such code will eventually fail as the promise here does not have a method.

Try executing this code, save it as `test.html` and run the file:

```
<!DOCTYPE html>
<html>
    <head>
        <script src="http://code.jquery.com/jquery-
        1.9.0.js"></script>
        <script>
            function getPromise(){
                return $.Deferred().promise();
            }

            try{
                getPromise().resolve("a");
            }
            catch(err){
            alert(err);
            }
        </script>
    </head>
    <body>
        <h1> you have seen the error.  </h1>
    </body>
</html>
```

You will get an error like this:

So, as mentioned earlier, it returns an object and with nearly the same interface as that of `Deferred`. However, it's there just to attach the callbacks not to resolve or reject; this is the catch that we talked about earlier. Now, how can we resolve it? Simple. You can use promise as a return value for another function; let's try the following code:

```html
<!DOCTYPE html>
<html>
    <head>
        <script src="http://code.jquery.com/jquery-
        1.9.0.js"></script>
        <script>
            var post = $.ajax({
                url: "/localhost/json/",
                data: {json: JSON.stringify({firstMovieName:
                "Terminator", secondMovieName: "Terminator 2"})} ,
                type: "POST"
            });

            post.done (function(p){
                alert(p.firstMovieName +  " saved.");
            });

            post.fail (function(){
                alert("error! b/c this URL is not functioning");
            });

        </script>
    </head>
    <body>
        <h1> you have seen the error.  </h1>
    </body>
</html>
```

When you run the preceding code, it will give you an error in the alert dialog box on the page, which it shouldn't when the URL passed in the URL variable is real. For the sake of understanding, let's assume the URL was proper and that it saved the value, the result will be like this:

The preceding code and the one before that has only one difference—you can add as many callbacks as you want, the grammar of the code is clean as it shows that we don't want an extra parameter in the method. Thus, you can ask promise in jQuery to perform some operations.

Projecting a promise in jQuery

In some cases, we have to just display the name of a promise. This will be much needed when you only want to see what the element can be or what operations you want to perform on an object. Using jQuery, we can easily achieve it by using the `pipe()` function.

Consider this code where we are projecting the result, which is an actor:

```html
<!DOCTYPE html>
<html>
    <head>
        <script src="http://code.jquery.com/jquery-
        1.9.0.js"></script>
        <script>
            var post = $.post("/echo/json/",
              {
                  json: JSON.stringify({firstName: "Arnold",
                  lastName: "Schwarzenegger"})
              }
            ).pipe(function(p){
              return "Name Saved >> " + p.firstName + "   " +
              p.lastName;
            });
```

```
            post.done(function(r){ alert(r); });
        </script>
    </head>
    <body>
        <h1> you have seen the result .   </h1>
    </body>
</html>
```

The result of the code will be the full name, Arnold Schwarzenegger, displayed on an alert dialog box at the browser:

As you can see, the projection of the result is an actor name used as an object. So, instead of deferred of a person, we have a deferred of Name Saved >> Arnold Schwarzenegger.

The pipe function can also be used to return the object from deep inside a method call. We can dig out an actor name and his IMDB rating, as explained in the following code:

```
<!DOCTYPE html>
<html>
    <head>
        <script src="http://code.jquery.com/jquery-
        1.9.0.js"></script>
        <script>
            function getActorById(customerId){
                return $.post("/echo/json/", {
                        json: JSON.stringify({firstName: "Arnold",
                        lastName: "Schwarzenegger", rating: "8.0"})
                }).pipe(function(p){
                    return p.rating;
                });
            }
```

```
function getRating(rating){
    return $.post("/echo/json/", {
            json: JSON.stringify({
                rating: "8.0" })
    }).pipe(function(p){
        return p.rating;
    });

}

function getActorRatingById(id){
    return getActorById)
            .pipe(getRating);
}


getActorRatingById(123)
    .done(function(a){
        alert("The rating of Actor is " + a);
    });

    </script>
</head>
<body>
    <h1> you have seen the result .  </h1>
</body>
</html>
```

When you run this code, it will give you an alert output on the browser, which will look like this:

By the virtue of `pipe()`, we will dig into callback and on passing the correct parameters to the function `getActorById()`; we able to get our desired results displayed. In a similar manner, you can use `pipe()` to reject `deferred` inside the callback.

One more thing that you can do with `pipe` is recursive deferred. Say, you have an asynchronous operation at the backend of API calls, and you need to poll all the response sets before you can put them to use. You can ask `pipe()` to help you out.

Consider the following code that will help collect API responses and let you know whether all the responses are collected or not:

```html
<!DOCTYPE html>
<html>
    <head>
        <script src="http://code.jquery.com/jquery-
        1.9.0.js"></script>
        <script>
            function getStatus(){
                var d = $.Deferred();
                $.post(
                    "/echo/json/",
                    {
                        json: JSON.stringify( {status:
                        Math.floor(Math.random()*4+1)} ),
                        delay: 1
                    }
                ).done(function(s){
                    d.resolve(s.status);
                }).fail(d.reject);
                return d.promise();
            }

            function pollApiCallDone(){
                //do something
                return getStatus()
                        .pipe(function(s){
                            if(s === 1 || s == 2) {
                                return s;
                            }

                            return pollApiCallDone();
                        });
            }
```

```
$.blockUI({message: "Please wait while we are  Loading
the results"});

pollApiCallDone()
    .pipe(function(s){
            switch(s){
            case 1:
                return "completed";
            case 2:
                return "not completed";
            }
    })
    .done(function(s){
        $.unblockUI();
        alert("The status of collection of API call is
        >>> " + s);
    });

    </script>
  </head>
  <body>
    <h1> you have seen the result .  </h1>
  </body>
</html>
```

Please note that we didn't give any hardcoded value for computing the results, rather we used math.random() to calculate the results every time we hit refresh. This is just a mechanism using which you can pool data, validate it, and then use it as required.

So, we saw how the pipe() method can be beneficial in writing neat and maintainable code. This also gave us a view of how we can use deferred in the longer run while remaining under the umbrella of jQuery.

Joining promises with $.when

$.when is another method that can accept multiple promises and return a master deferred object. This master object can be resolved if all the promises are resolved, or it would be rejected if any of the promises were rejected. You may have sequence like when().then().done() or you can add multiple when() methods followed by then() and done().

Let's take a look at an example of how the code will look like with `$when()`:

```html
<!DOCTYPE html>
<html>
  <head>
    <script src="http://code.jquery.com/jquery-
    1.9.0.js"></script>
    <script>
      function getActorByRating(id){
      var d = $.Deferred();
      $.post(
        "/echo/json/",
        {json: JSON.stringify({firstName: "Arnold",
        lastName: "Schwarzenegger", rating: "8.0"})}
      ).done(function(p){
        d.resolve(p);
      }).fail(d.reject);
      return d.promise();
      }

      function getActorById(rating){
      return $.post("/echo/json/", {
          json: JSON.stringify({
              rating: "8.0"})
      }).pipe(function(p){
        return p.rating;
      });
      }

      $.when(getActorByRating(123), getActorById("123456789"))
      .done(function(person, rating){
        alert("The name is " + person.firstName + " and the
        rating is " + rating);
      });
    </script>
  </head>
  <body>
    <h1> you have seen the result .  </h1>
  </body>
</html>
```

When you execute the preceding code, it will generate an output like this:

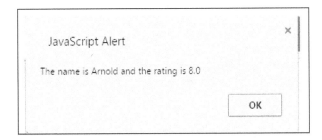

Notice that at the end of the code, the $.when function returns a new master deferred object, and we used two results in one done() callback.

We also changed the getActorByRating() method due to the fact that the promise of an AJAX call, which has the content payload, has the first element in the result along with status code included.

However, this is not the end; you can also use $.when with pipes. Let's see how:

```
<!DOCTYPE html>
<html>
    <head>
        <script src="http://code.jquery.com/jquery-
        1.9.0.js"></script>
        <script>
            function getActor(id){
                var d = $.Deferred();
                $.post(
                    "/echo/json/",
                    {json: JSON.stringify({firstName: "Arnold",
                    lastName: "Schwarzenegger", rating: "8.0"})}
                ).done(function(p){
                    d.resolve(p);
                }).fail(d.reject);
                return d.promise();
            }

            function getPersonByRating(rating){
                return $.post("/echo/json/", {
                        json: JSON.stringify({
                            rating: "8.0" })
                }).pipe(function(p){
```

```
                return p.rating;
            });
        }


        $.when(getActor(123), getPersonByRating("123456789"))
            .pipe(function(person, rating){
                return $.extend(person, {rating: rating});
            })
            .done(function(person){
                alert("The name is " + person.firstName + " and the
                rating is " + person.rating);
            });

    </script>
  </head>
  <body>
    <h1> you have seen the result .  </h1>
  </body>
</html>
```

From the preceding code, you can easily see how when() and pipe() can work in combination and produce results. By summarizing the preceding code, we can say the sequence of our code was like when(), pipe(), and done(). The done() method is the last milestone that has compiled and presented the result on our screen.

We can also use when() as an operator. Remember in JavaScript, every method can be a variable. Let's see how to do it using this code:

```
<!DOCTYPE html>
<html>
    <head>
        <script src="http://code.jquery.com/jquery-
        1.9.0.js"></script>
        <script>
            function getActor(id){
                var d = $.Deferred();
                $.post(
                    "/echo/json/",
                    {json: JSON.stringify({firstName: "Arnold",
                    lastName: "Schwarzenegger", rating: "8.0"}),
                     delay: 4}
                ).done(function(p){
                    d.resolve(p);
                }).fail(d.reject);
                return d.promise();
```

```
        }

        function getActorByRating(rating){
            return $.post("/echo/json/", {
                    json: JSON.stringify({
                                    rating: "8.0"
                                }),
                    delay: 2
            }).pipe(function(p){
                return p.rating;
            });
        }


        function load(){
            $.blockUI({message: "Loading..."});
            var loading = getActor(123)
                .done(function(c){
                    $("span#firstName").html(c.firstName)
                });

            var loadingRating = getActorByRating("8.0")
                .done(function(rating){
                    $("span#rating").html(rating)
                });

            $.when(loading, loadingRating)
                .done($.unblockUI);
        }

        load();

    </script>
  </head>
  <body>
    <h1> you have seen the result .  </h1>
  </body>
</html>
```

So from the preceding code, you can clearly see how we can use when() in many different ways. We can add more variety to it as it has many implementations and best case scenarios for solving complex problems.

Your own $.Deferred process

You can customize the deferred object as per your need. This is simple and can be achieved by calling out the `jQuery.Deferred()` method. We can also define our own process and the sequence of the flow and arrange the output as required. We can use `setInterval()` to set up the delays and `setTimeout()` to decide when to end the sequence. The scope of variable declaration decides whether the deferred object has to be locally or globally processed. If the deferred object is assigned to a local variable, we can call deferred object's `resolve()`, `promise()`, and `notify()` events.

Let's have a look at this example:

```
var myCustomPromise = process();
myCustomPromise.done(function() {
    $('#result').html('done.');
});
myCustomPromise.progress(function() {
    $('#result').html($('#result').html() + '.');
});

function process() {
    var deferred = $.Deferred();

    MyTimerCall = setInterval(function() {
        deferred.notify();
    }, 1000);

    setTimeout(function() {
        clearInterval(MyTimerCall);
        deferred.resolve();
    }, 10000);

    return deferred.myCustomPromise();
}
```

So, from the preceding code, we are able to achieve a skeleton of the processes. This can be simplified by making it more concise or by adding some combining methods such as `then()`, `when()`, and so on.

Let's have a look at this compact code:

```
var MyTimerCall;

(function process() {
```

```
$('#result').html('waiting…');
var deferred = $.Deferred();

MyTimerCall = setInterval(function() {
  deferred.notify();
}, 1000);

setTimeout(function() {
    clearInterval(MyTimerCall);
    deferred.resolve();
}, 10000);

return deferred.promise();
})().then(function() { $('#result').html('done.'); },
      null,
      function() { $('#result').
      html($('#result').html() + '.'); });
```

This is more concise and easy to scale. The learning element from this section is one thing; you can also go for the custom-made deferred in jQuery. It's easy, maintainable, and you can scale it as per your need.

The advent of promises in jQuery

So far we learned how promise can be used in jQuery, what deferred object is, and how we can achieve certain tasks using this concept. Why should we use it? The answer is simple, it has many capabilities to maximize our output and build applications in a lesser time. However, what can it actually do for us? Let's have a look.

We can call the `done()` and `fail()` functions as many times as we want, with different callbacks. Maybe we have a callback function that can halt our animation, or one that does a new AJAX call, and so on:

```
var promise = $.ajax({
  url: "/echo/"
});

promise.done(StopFadeFunction);
promise.done(FormAjaxFunction);
promise.done(ShowIErrorFunction);
promise.fail(GetErrorFunction);
```

No matter whether the AJAX call has finished, we can still call the `done()` and `fail()` functions and the callbacks are executed immediately. So, variables stated are not a big deal. When the call has finished, it will end up in either the success state or the failed state, and this state will not change.

We can combine promises. Say we have to do two simultaneous AJAX calls and we need to execute a function when both are successfully finished, as shown in the following code:

```
$.when() function.
var promise1 = $.ajax("/echo1");
var promise2 = $.ajax("/echo2");
$.when(promise1, promise2).done(function(Obj1, Obj2) {
    // place object handler here
});
```

From jQuery 1.8, we can chain the `then()` function consecutively:

```
var promiseOne = $.ajax("/echo1");

function getSomthing () {
    return $.ajax("/echo2");
}
promiseOne.then(getSomthing).then(function(customeServerScript){
    // Both promises are resolved
});
```

Summary

So, with this chapter coming to an end, let's revise the topics we have covered so far.

We have seen the how jQuery has started taking shape and how it became a fundamental element of the modern-day web development. We have learned how to build basic jQuery documents and how to call the functions embedded into HTML files. We have learned why we started using deferred and promise in jQuery and how it helped us in achieving cutting-edge applications on both web -based platform and portable devices. We have seen saw many working examples to understand better and clear any doubts. The topic of promises in jQuery is huge, but we tried to summarize as much as we can to lay out solid foundations for those who hadn't used this property before and to help those who are already using it.

In the next chapter, we will see how all the combined JavaScript and their properties are shaping up to bring the world closer and making our life easier in the days to come.

JavaScript – The Future Is Now

9

So far in the previous chapters, we focused on how to become indispensably good at applying the concept of promises in different JavaScript libraries and how we can get maximum advantages in our future projects. However, this is not all about JavaScript.

Although promises are huge and their implementations can bring a number of benefits, that's not the end of JavaScript. In fact, JavaScript has more to offer in the coming years than we can have even thought of. It is the progressive language of the modern age and it's gaining popularity day by day. What else can JavaScript offer us? We will try to find out in this chapter.

Let's start with ECMAScript 6.

ECMAScript 6 (ECMA 262)

ECMAScript Language Specification is in its sixth version. Since the time its first version was published in 1997, ECMAScript has become one of the world's most vastly adopted general purpose programming languages. It is known for its ability to embed itself in web browsers along with its ability to use server-side and embedded applications.

Many consider the sixth edition to be the most detailed and most widely covered update of ECMAScript since its inception in 1997.

We will consider the sixth edition of ECMA 262 for our discussion in this chapter; it's a draft version with the aims to include better support for large applications, library creation, and for the use of ECMAScript as a compilation target for other languages.

harmony:generators

harmony:generators are first class croutons that will be represented as objects, which will be encapsulating suspended execution contexts (that is, function activations). Till date, these are under review and can be changed, so we will just take these under consideration to gain knowledge about them.

A few high-level examples would be helpful in better understanding of what the shape of harmony will be after it gets approved.

Since these are unapproved drafts, we will use examples from the ECMAScript parent website.

The reference code to be used in this section can be found at http://wiki. ecmascript.org/doku.php?id=harmony:generators.

The Fibonacci series

The "infinite" sequence of Fibonacci numbers is:

```
Function* Fibonacci () {
    let [prev, curr] = [0, 1];
    For (;;) {
        [prev, curr] = [curr, prev + curr];
        yield curr;
    }
}
```

Generators can be iterated over in loops:

```
for (n of fibonacci()) {
    // truncate the sequence at 1000
    if (n > 1000)
        break;
    print(n);
}
```

Generators are iterators as shown in the following code:

```
let seq = fibonacci();
print(seq.next()); // 1
print(seq.next()); // 2
print(seq.next()); // 3
print(seq.next()); // 5
print(seq.next()); // 8
```

The preceding snippets are very high-level syntax, and there is a fair chance that they will be modified. Generators will be a key element and a remarkable addition to harmony but will take time to fully implement it.

The MEAN stack

Although the MEAN stack is not a new concept, this has provided us the base of everything in JavaScript. It provides you with a JavaScript-based web server in the form of Node.js, a database in the form of MongoDB, which also has JavaScript as the core language, Express.js as a Node.js web application framework, and Angular. js as the frontend element that can let you extend HTML in a more advanced and modern way.

The concepts have been around for a while, but they have the potential to grow beyond imagination. Imagine a full-scale financial application or an entire banking system based on the MEAN stack or controlling industries. The hardware will be utilizing services from this stack, but this will happen in the near future, which is not so late, but still it needs time to fully implement the stack.

The reason I am saying this is because the corporate sector is still reluctant in adopting the MEAN standard or moving towards it and the reason is the level of maturity and financial backup of these open source products. Also, they have to upgrade their existing infrastructure. Whatever the reason, modern day web apps are heavily using this stack for writing lightweight and scalable apps. Let's mark the MEAN stack as our item number one for the future of JavaScript.

Real-time communication in JavaScript

Another powerful feature that has been called the future of JavaScript is real-time communication between two sockets. Before JavaScript, socket programming had been around for so long that every major programming language had its version of reading and writing data using sockets, but with JavaScript, this is kind of a new concept that needs a lot of work at this stage. There are certain ways in which you can implement real-time socket programming in JavaScript, but the most mature way at the moment is by using Socket.IO.

It basically enables a two-way event-based communication in real time that will, in turn, make the communication between two entities possible. It supports a variety of platforms, which includes web browsers, handheld devices, mobile devices, and any other device that has the communication feature enabled. Its implementation is fairly easy and reliable with high quality and speed.

What can we achieve with this? Well, there are a number of possibilities, and it depends on how you can give them a try based on the support Socket.IO has to offer. At this point in time, you can write real-time analytics for your business intelligence or market predictions or trend identification, or you can use it for real-time media streaming from one part of the planet to other using its binary stream functions, or you can use it to monitor you premises from a remote location. All these implementations are available right now and such ideas can be brought to reality by using the functions smartly.

The conclusion is that Socket.IO is one of the most robust real-time communication libraries that you can rely on. Looking at the current trend, we can safely say that real-time communication between devices can be one of the greatest strengths of JavaScript in future. This doesn't really have to happen via Socket.IO; any library that has potential will dominate. It's about the concept of how JavaScript will impress us in the near future.

Internet of Things

Not too long ago, hardware interfacing with devices and machines was only limited to certain mature and developed programming languages, and no one gave any thought to whether JavaScript would be able to stand in the same line as these mature languages. It was a status quo limited to C++ or Java or some other high-level languages, but this is not the case anymore.

With more focus on JavaScript, developers and engineers are now trying to use the power of JavaScript in hardware interfacing. They are overcoming the problems of JavaScript by writing down intelligent code and by utilizing libraries that are already using communication to a device to some extent.

One such effort is called Raspberry Pi. Let's talk about Raspberry Pi and its purpose, then we will take a look at how JavaScript is using it.

Raspberry Pi is a simple credit card-type computer design to learn programming in a very simple and effective manner. It comes with a board that you can call a computer without any peripherals attached. You have to attach the mouse, keyboard, and a screen to bring it to life. It has an operating system mounted on an SD card and is open for experiments. This is portable and you can attach any device to it or program another device using it. It has all the basic elements that a computer must have, but in a very simple, portable, and easy-to-handle manner.

Now, what does it have to do with JavaScript? Well, JavaScript is now everywhere, so its implementation has also started for Raspberry Pi with Pijs.io.

Like you can write in any other language for Raspberry Pi, you can also use JavaScript to write applications of your handheld computer. This JavaScript library will allow you to interact with hardware using JavaScript and program devices for your needs. You can see the library at `http://pijs.io/`.

As discussed earlier, hardware interfacing is not limited to Raspberry Pi; any other implementations that are out there must be doing the same thing. The core of these lines is to show how powerful JavaScript is becoming and how widely it is accepted. Now, people are considering it for programming their devices, regardless of whether these devices belong to their daily use or commercial use. The future of JavaScript in computer hardware interfacing is very bright and it's growing rapidly.

Computer animation and in 3D graphics

In 1996, a whole new concept of **computer generated images** (**CGI**) was introduced in the revolutionary movie, *Toy Story*. This movie had set new standards in animation and computer graphics. The success of the movie was not just due to its screenplay but also due to the technology used to build it.

In the current time, the field of computer animation has developed from many aspects and is still growing at a rapid speed. So, what does JavaScript have to do with all these advancements? Well, JavaScript is getting readier than ever before to play its role in computer animated and 3D graphics via the Web.

WebGL is an open source JavaScript API for rendering 2D and 3D images and objects. The power of WebGL lies in its extension to nearly every browser by adopting the standards of browsers and their engines. It's highly adaptable and can be used in any modern day web browser to render images as required.

By the virtue of WebGL, it's now possible to write interactive and cutting edge games that require no additional plug-in to run. It will also help in the future to see animated computer modeling with a browser rather than using heavy, costly, and bulky software. It will also help in visualizing information on the go. So, you can see the visual impact of stock prices when they go up and down to other stocks where you have invested.

So far, WebGL has gained support from all the key players of the industry that includes Apple for its Safari; Microsoft for its IE 11 and its later release, the Edge browser; Google for its Chrome browser; and Mozilla for its Firefox. Also, note here that WebGL is the brainchild of Vladimir Vukićević of Mozilla, who released its initial version in 2011.

We can conclude with the fact that JavaScript has planted seeds in animated and 3D graphics as well, and in the near future, this will not only help JavaScript to gain credibility to, but will also bring ease to many developers and engineers who have to learn new languages every time they face a limitation in their current language pack. With a unified language, the output apps will be more interesting.

NoSQL databases

There was a time when knowing RDBMS was a must for all developers, especially for those who were working on database-driven applications. The expectation was that you must know what primary keys were, what joins were, how to normalize databases, and what entity-relationship diagrams were. However, slowly this scenario is fading and a new concept of NoSQL is emerging in today's world, where vast data-driven applications are still in play.

Before we move forward, let's talk about why engineers are focusing on non-RDBMS technologies. The reason is simple. Data-driven applications have grown in a tremendous way and they're generating terabytes of data around the world in every hour of the day. To process such data and get the desired result is not an easy task. **Database Administrators (DBAs)** write a query and execute it to fetch the data from distributed repositories of databases, they have to wait for several hours to know whether the results are printed on their screen or a slight error in placing the operator has destroyed all their efforts. This is because of the way RDBMS was designed, but in today's modern world, such delays and computing times cost you a fortune and your reputation.

What is the alternative then? NoSQL databases! In an earlier section of this chapter, we already saw that MongoDB played a key role in the MEAN stack. However, it's worth giving MongoDB a few more lines here as it's our candidate for the future growth of JavaScript.

What is MongoDB? It's a document-oriented NoSQL database with cross-platform adaptability with JSON such as documents. Till February 2015, it was the fourth most popular DBMS in the world and is considered to be the most popular data store in the world.

Why have we listed MongoDB in our candidates for future JavaScript growth? Simply because it's JavaScript-based and you can write scripts within its console in pure JavaScript. This makes it a highly adaptable DB technology based in JavaScript. The way it's progressing, it will not only obsolete current scenario of RDBMS but also will do wonders when combined with the rest of the MEAN stack or hardware interfacing or the Web or with Socket.IO.

In any shape, MongoDB will help the rest of the applications to grow in the future and also transform the existing RDBMS to more accessible and quick responder engines.

Summary

In this chapter, we learned that JavaScript is a game changer and that it has a bright future ahead. JavaScript has a great tendency and adaptability, which will lead it to the next level of usage in almost every domain of computer science. The possibilities are limitless, and the sky is the limit for JavaScript. In the near future, JavaScript will dominate every other programming language due to its adaptability, acceptability, and contributions of thousands of developers and committed software giants.

With this, we come to the end of this book.

Let's recap what we learned in this book. At the beginning, we took a deep dive into what JavaScript is and from where it began, what the structure of JavaScript is and how different browsers are using it. We also saw different programming models and the one that is being used by JavaScript.

Then, our journey took a bend towards the core of this book, Promises.js. We learned a great deal about the basics of promises that has taken us towards the advanced usages of this concept. We then saw it with respect to different technologies and also samples the code to clear out any ambiguities.

So, all in all, this book is not only about promises in JavaScript, but it has a solid overview of the history, implementation, and usages of JavaScript and promises. With this book, you can not only become a master in promises, but also retain a unique level of understanding, thus implementing this concept in much brighter and numerous ways.

Happy learning!

Index

Symbols

$.Deferred process 148
$.deferred().promise(), in jQuery 136-139
$.when method
  promises, joining with 143-147

A

Android Deferred Object
  defining 53
  failure callbacks, for task 54
  object success, for task 54
  several promises, merging 54
  URL 54
Angular.js
  concurrency 121, 122
  defining 105
  evolution 103, 104
  promises, implementing 117
  URL 105
  using 104
  using, on local machine 106, 107
Angular.js directive 104
Angular.js document
  structure 104, 105
Angular.js file
  creating 105
  HTML 5 doc, creating 105
  JavaScript file, adding 106
application logic
  decoupling 35
arguments
  passing 119, 120
Asynchronous JavaScript and
    XML (AJAX) 2

asynchronous programming
  using, problems 67
asynchronous programming model
  about 11, 12
  blocking programs, defining 12, 13
  defining 26
  densities, defining with 12
  threads, using 13

B

base repository, WinJS
  URL 65
binding 5
BlockingQueue interface
  implementations 46
bootstrap
  URL 108

C

callback 29
callback-based promise
  versus Q-based promise 90
callbacks, in JavaScript
  basic rules, for implementing 17
  function, blocking in humans 16
  handling 17, 18
  working 17
call stream 5
compatibility, event
  URL 21
components, java.util.concurrent
  about 45
  Executor 45
  Queues 46

composed promise 120
computer animation
  about 155
  in 3D graphics 155
computer generated images (CGI) 155
Concurrent packages
  classes 47
CountDownLatch class
  about 47
  URL 47
createFileAsync method 72
CSS3 66
CyclicBarrier class
  about 47
  URL 47

D

Database Administrator (DBA) 156
deferred
  about 30
  working 30
Deferred, in jQuery 135, 136
deferred objects 120
delay 91
distribution history, WinJS
  WinJS 1.0 65
  WinJS 2.0 for Windows 8.1 65
  WinJS 3.0 65
  WinJS Phone 2.1 for Windows Phone 8.1 65
  WinJS Xbox 1.0 for Windows 65
Document Object Model (DOM) 20
DOM 2 event specification
  URL 22
done() function
  defining 71
done() method 146

E

ECMAScript 6 (ECMA 262) 151
elements, Angular.js
  about 107
  data, filtering 110, 111
  scope data, supplying 108-110
  scopes, controlling 112, 113
  views, routing 114-116

environment
  selecting 78
  setting up, for Node.js 79
error
  and success, combination 123
error handling 69, 70
event handling
  defining 19
  DOM 20
events
  about 19
  decoupling 35
  event handling, mechanism 19
  form events 22
  functions, triggering in response
    to events 21
  interface events 22
  Microsoft events 22
  mouse events 22
  Mozilla events 22
  types 21
  W3C events 22
events handlers
  about 20
  onblur 21
  onchange 21
  onclick 20
  ondblclick 20
  Onerror 20
  onfocus 21
  onkeydown 21
  Onkeypress 21
  onkeyup 21
  Onload 20
  onmousedown 20
  Onmouseout 20
  onmouseover 20
  onmouseup 20
  onreset 21
  onselect 21
  onsubmit 21
  Onunload 20
  URL 21
events, in JavaScript
  defining 21
example, jQuery
  about 132

Thank you for buying
Mastering JavaScript Promises

About Packt Publishing

Packt, pronounced 'packed', published its first book, *Mastering phpMyAdmin for Effective MySQL Management*, in April 2004, and subsequently continued to specialize in publishing highly focused books on specific technologies and solutions.

Our books and publications share the experiences of your fellow IT professionals in adapting and customizing today's systems, applications, and frameworks. Our solution-based books give you the knowledge and power to customize the software and technologies you're using to get the job done. Packt books are more specific and less general than the IT books you have seen in the past. Our unique business model allows us to bring you more focused information, giving you more of what you need to know, and less of what you don't.

Packt is a modern yet unique publishing company that focuses on producing quality, cutting-edge books for communities of developers, administrators, and newbies alike. For more information, please visit our website at www.packtpub.com.

About Packt Open Source

In 2010, Packt launched two new brands, Packt Open Source and Packt Enterprise, in order to continue its focus on specialization. This book is part of the Packt Open Source brand, home to books published on software built around open source licenses, and offering information to anybody from advanced developers to budding web designers. The Open Source brand also runs Packt's Open Source Royalty Scheme, by which Packt gives a royalty to each open source project about whose software a book is sold.

Writing for Packt

We welcome all inquiries from people who are interested in authoring. Book proposals should be sent to author@packtpub.com. If your book idea is still at an early stage and you would like to discuss it first before writing a formal book proposal, then please contact us; one of our commissioning editors will get in touch with you.

We're not just looking for published authors; if you have strong technical skills but no writing experience, our experienced editors can help you develop a writing career, or simply get some additional reward for your expertise.

Mastering JavaScript High Performance

ISBN:978-1-78439-729-6   Paperback: 208 pages

Master the art of building, deploying, and optimizing faster web applications with JavaScript

1. Test and optimize JavaScript code efficiently.

2. Build faster and more proficient JavaScript programs for web browsers and hybrid mobile apps.

3. Step-by-step tutorial stuffed with real-world examples.

Mastering jQuery

ISBN: 978-1-78398-546-3   Paperback: 400 pages

Elevate your development skills by leveraging every available ounce of jQuery

1. Create and decouple custom event types to efficiently use them and suit your users' needs.

2. Incorporate custom, optimized versions of the jQuery library into your pages to maximize the efficiency of your website.

3. Get the most out of jQuery by gaining exposure to real-world examples with tricks and tips to enhance your skills.

Please check **www.PacktPub.com** for information on our titles

**JavaScript Mobile Application
Development**

ISBN: 978-1-78355-417-1   Paperback: 332 pages

Create neat cross-platform mobile apps using Apache
Cordova and jQuery Mobile

1. Configure your Android, iOS, and Window
   Phone 8 development environments.

2. Extend the power of Apache Cordova
   by creating your own Apache Cordova
   cross-platform mobile plugins.

3. Enhance the quality and the robustness of
   your Apache Cordova mobile application
   by unit testing its logic using Jasmine.

JavaScript Promises Essentials

ISBN: 978-1-78398-564-7   Paperback: 90 pages

Build fully functional web applications using
Promises, the new standard in JavaScript

1. Integrate JavaScript Promises into your
   application by mastering the key concepts
   of the Promises API.

2. Replace complex nested callbacks in JavaScript
   with the more intuitive chained Promises.

3. Acquire the knowledge needed to start working
   with JavaScript Promises immediately.

Please check **www.PacktPub.com** for information on our titles